YOUCAT

Confirmation Book

YOUCAT

ENGLISH

CONFIRMATION BOOK

Edited by

YOUCAT Team, Augsburg
Bernhard Meuser
Nils Baer

Translated by Frank Davidson

IGNATIUS PRESS SAN FRANCISCO

Original German Edition:
YOUCAT (Deutsch) Firmbuch
© 2011 Pattloch Verlag GmbH & Co. KG, Munich.
All rights reserved

Cover design, layout, illustrations and typesetting:
Alexander von Lengerke, Cologne
Overall production: Auer Buch + Medien GmbH, Donauwörth

The trademark YOUCAT is used with the kind permission of the publisher of
YOUCAT—Youth Catechism of the Catholic Church www.youcat.org

© 2014 by Ignatius Press, San Francisco
All rights reserved
ISBN 978-1-58617-835-2
Library of Congress Control Number 2014903122
Printed in the United States of America ∞

20 19 18 17 16 15 14 13 12 11 10 9 8 7 6 5 4 3 2 1

Content

1

MARATHON AND CONFIRMATION

Getting Started

Hi!

Suppose you want to run a marathon—in New York, say, or in London. You won't succeed without training. You have to start running at least half a year in advance. Then you're going to have to start upping the tempo and the distance. And if you're really going to be serious about it, then maybe you'll even need to change your diet, to give up those yummy French fries and those irresistible chocolate bars. The reward you get for your effort is the feeling of how, week by week, your body starts to feel finer and fitter. Then finally the day of the race arrives. Others are soon gasping for breath, but you seem to have all the energy you need and find yourself well to the front of the field.

→ 300
Why do we have to work to form our character?

It's a little bit like that with this Confirmation course that you have started on. Here, too, you need to start at least half a year beforehand in order to be really geared up for a very big event. Maybe you're saying to yourself now: "What, run a marathon—that would be crazy! But Confirmation—I'll get that anyway, so why make more effort than I have to?" Okay, so let's make the comparison:

Marathon and Confirmation

With a **marathon** it's your physical strength that is being tested	In **Confirmation** it's important to prepare your soul, your inner self
In a **marathon** you draw on your own reserves of strength	In **Confirmation** you take divine power into yourself (on which you can later draw)
A **marathon** increases your self-confidence as a person	In **Confirmation** God himself affirms your identity as his beloved child and co-worker

Obviously, you can't really compare running a marathon with receiving Confirmation. You can choose to run a marathon, or you can choose not to. And the truth is, it doesn't matter in the least whether you ran in London or New York, whether you came in 1st or 577th or last of all—or, in fact, whether you even ever ran a marathon in the first place.

→ 34

What should you do once you have come to know God?

But not to seek God even though you know that he exists— that is simply crazy! Completely wrong! And that's the point of Confirmation: You have a unique opportunity to discover God, to open your heart to him, and to let him come right up close to you.

1.2 Fully wired for power

Have you heard of Mother Teresa? She was a great holy woman who gave her life to the poorest of the poor and did not shrink from tenderly nursing beggars and outcasts, even the infectious, diseased, and dying ones. Whenever she had a spare moment of time, on a train or a plane maybe, she would snatch up a scrap of paper and, in her wobbly handwriting, scribble down a few important things about God, things from which we can learn a lot.

This is the note she once made (she didn't write "Confirmation" at the top, but that's exactly what she meant):

Often you can see power lines running alongside the street. Unless current is flowing through them, there is no light. The power line is you and I! The current is God! We have the power either to allow the current to flow through us and thus to generate the light of the world: JESUS—or to refuse to be used and thus to allow the darkness to spread.

Five powerful sentences. All you need to know ... Read them over three times! Or five times! Or ten times! If you have completely understood them, then you can ring up your bishop this very moment and say, "Please confirm me! Immediately! I have understood everything!" But maybe that would be a bit like ringing up your trainer and telling him, "I've figured out the secret of the marathon. Put my name down for New York right away!" Your trainer would probably turn around and laugh and then ask: "So how many races have you actually run? How many miles have you run so far?" And you would have to answer, "Well, none, actually ..." You would feel a fool; in fact, you might even lose heart and give up on your great dream. In reality, of course, every big journey begins with the first step. If you want to become a professional marathon runner, then you'd better get your running shoes out of the basement tonight and set your alarm for early tomorrow morning. Otherwise it will never happen.

→ 301

How does a person become prudent?

1.3 Do you want to feel the power of God within you?

It's the same with Confirmation. Is the current flowing within you? Do you have an intense connection with God? Or do you believe it isn't possible? Do you maybe feel at the moment more like a length of dead cable, lying there with no current passing through it? Do you long to be a channel through which divine Love can flow? Do you want to feel the power of God within you? Do you want to live a strong and worthwhile life? Did you ever have the feeling of being very close to God, of being very near, very loved, protected, carried, led? Or maybe you have to admit to yourself, in all honesty: I feel a great emptiness inside; right now I can't really say I've got that much power running through me ...

→ 290

How does God help us to be free men?

 → 287

But doesn't "freedom" consist of being able to choose evil as well?

Okay, we can all be like religious couch potatoes sometimes; we can hang around aimlessly, sit there complaining, chill out endlessly. We can sit there at our laptop and kid ourselves that we don't feel that inner emptiness. We can let ourselves be willingly enslaved, stay up till the wee small hours with our noses stuck to the screen, watch bad films, get hooked on computer games, drag like an addict at a cigarette, or spend our lives like some sort of outgrowth of Facebook.

But that is not what God has made us for.

 → 1

For what purpose are we here on earth?

1.4 **God—as your Coach**

God wants us to be strong, proud, and free, no one's slave, but God's alone, glowing with an inner light, loving, warmhearted, attentive, and creative; fighters for good and resistance fighters against the whisperings of Satan, watchful guardians of an endangered creation, faithful friends to the poor and persecuted, and more, and more, and more …

Does that take your breath away?

If you really want to have a life of strength like that, if you want this for yourself, if you want it with God's help, then all I can say is:

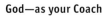

What a training schedule! You are ready to start on the road to your Confirmation. But you need to be aware that a marathon is child's play in comparison.

→ 203
What is Confirmation?

The aim of this book is to be your coach and go with you right up to the big day of your Confirmation. You'll find many tips in it for leading an exciting life with God, but above all you'll find lots of sidebars pointing you to two books you'll be constantly using during this course—the BIBLE and YOUCAT.

1.5 The Bible and YOUCAT

Of the two books, the Bible is by far the more important, for it is "God's Word". Sure, the Bible, too, was written by men, but these were men filled with the Holy Spirit. "Ignorance of the Scriptures is ignorance of Christ," says St. Jerome, and St. Francis of Assisi adds, "Reading the Holy Scriptures is seeking advice from Christ."

YOUCAT is the youth catechism of the Catholic Church— basically something like a down-to-earth handbook of our faith. Take a moment to read the challenging foreword to this book, by Pope Emeritus Benedict XVI, in which he speaks directly to young people like you. He tells you there:

> You need to know what you believe. You need to know your faith with that same precision with which an IT specialist knows the inner workings of a computer. You need to understand it like a good musician knows the piece he is playing.

→ 21
Faith—what is it?

The great thing about YOUCAT is that this youth catechism was written in collaboration with a group of around 50 young people aged between 15 and 25. They were able to introduce their own questions; they also contributed the best of their own photos and wanted to have cartoon characters in the book. It was these young people who also came up with the crazy flipbook idea. Try it out some time! Or read up on what

Confirmation has to do with a football match, and faith with parachute jumping.

1.6 **Four steps—the training plan**

Right, then, now for the training program! It's a demanding one, but then, as you know: no pain, no gain ... Just stick to the "four steps" below, which will help you immensely to advance in your training for a life with God.

1 Stay with the course

Don't miss a single session of your Confirmation course! After all, you wouldn't miss a training session if you wanted to run the New York Marathon, would you?

→ 219

How often must a Catholic Christian participate in the celebration of the Eucharist?

2 Try to stay close to God

Go to Holy Mass every Sunday! Don't miss. Ever. Come rain, come shine. Whether you had a party the night before, or need your brunch on Sunday morning. Holy Mass is a date with God. Unless you are very sick, that's something you don't miss.

→ 499

When should a person pray?

3 Talk to God

The bedside rule. That is: in the morning don't go beyond the bedside without saying morning prayers; and at night time don't go beyond the bedside without saying your night-time prayers. No one can build a relationship with God without talking to him—and prayer is nothing else than this. Most important of all is the **OUR FATHER**, but the

HAIL MARY is important, too. And look in the Bible sometime for the Psalms—they are some of the most beautiful prayers ever written. Take time for your own prayers, too; talk to God straight from the heart.

Listen to God's Word

See to it that you get hold of a Bible! Perhaps you can ask for a nice copy as a present. The Bible is a bit like a rather long letter from God to you. Try and read a little of it regularly, perhaps during your vacation. It's best to start with the New Testament, with the Gospels. Try and understand what God is saying to you through his Word.

Phew, that's enough to start with. And now, all the best with your YOUCAT Confirmation course!

On behalf of the YOUCAT team,

Nils Baer and Bernhard Meuser

 → YOUCAT → Bible

In the margin you will find numerous references to the numbered questions in YOUCAT. Have a copy at hand and look up the references if you find anything not quite clear. You'll also find references to important Bible verses, which you can likewise look up in the Bible. Usually it's very important to check the context, what comes before and after.

Why many people don't want to know about God

No doubt some people have already told you:

GOD doesn't exist! God is merely an invention.

Many people have a strange interest in saying that God does not exist. Why are they so aggressive toward God, wanting everything that reminds us of him to disappear from the world? Surely, it should be a matter of total indifference to them? Perhaps they don't want to know about God because then they would have to change their lives completely. If God does exist, if God is absolute goodness and desires nothing else but

→ 357

Is atheism
always a sin
against God?

THERE'S PROBABLY NO GOD.
NOW STOP WORRYING AND ENJOY YOUR LIFE.

goodness, then it is absolutely impossible to lie, to commit adultery, take drugs, cheat others, and regard ourselves as the center of the universe. That is, it is impossible to do these things without ultimately having to face the consequences of such actions.

Again, many people call themselves atheists simply because they think it is more cool to be, so to speak, their own "god" and to decide for themselves what is good and bad. But someone who puts his own ego at the center of everything is simply an egotist.

→ 5

Why do people
deny that God
exists, if they
can know him by
reason?

We have all met such egotists from time to time, and they tend to be rather unpleasant people. Such people are implicitly atheists, for it is clear that in their world view there can be no one bigger, better, cleverer, more beautiful, or more deserving than they are themselves.

(He made
... men ...)
that they should
seek God, in the
hope that they
might feel after
him and find him.
Yet he is not far
from each one of
us, for 'In him we
live and move and
have our being.'

Acts 17:27–28

→ 41

Does science
make the Creator
superfluous?

→ 42

Can someone
accept the theory
of evolution and
still believe in the
Creator?

2.2 And what if I can't find God?

But there are also people who are by no means ego-tistical and yet still do not believe in God. They often say, I can't find God; he is nowhere to be found. Perhaps it would help them to stop and think very carefully. It is a matter of log-ic—and for this we need to engage our little gray brain cells, and engage them 100% (hence the following page is only for people who can really think straight):

1. Everything we see in the universe has a cause, a reason it exists. I exist because my parents gave life to me. The rocky cliffs on the coast exist because of movements in the earth's crust over millions of years that caused the land to be raised higher than the sea. For each thing we see around us, there must be something else that gave rise to it.

2. The universe (the totality of things and beings existing in space and time) also exists.

3. Hence there must necessarily be something that is the cause/the reason for the existence of the universe. It would be totally illogical to assume that the mouse, the ocean, and the stars all have a cause for their existence but that the universe does not have such a cause. Even the universe as a whole cannot exist "without cause".

4. The cause or reason for the universe as a whole must, how-ever, be greater than, and above all entirely different from,

the universe itself and everything within it. What has brought forth both space and time cannot itself be a part of space and time.

5. This "something" that is greater than everything in the world and that must necessarily exist, since otherwise the universe itself would be without cause, we call **GOD**.

2.3 The miracle of the little grain of sand

TEST IT for yourself: Try for a moment to imagine "nothing"—in other words, absolute nothingness, not even a kind of darkness or a great emptiness—no: really, absolutely, nothing. Nothing, nothing, nothing! Not even thinking. Simply nothing.

Bet you don't succeed! The philosopher Leibniz once said that there is only one great question in the world:

Why is there anything at all, and not simply nothing?

🔥 The fact is, the one thing we actually simply cannot imagine—namely, nothing—is the one thing that should be self-evident. The normal thing to assume would be that there is simply nothing, and there's an end to it!

 → 43
Is the world a product of chance?

🔥 But in fact there is something. We know this with absolute certainty. And even if there were only a single tiny grain of sand and nothing else—even that would be an incredible miracle. For one single tiny grain of sand alone would destroy "nothingness".

🔥 There must be someone there who has uttered his great "Yes" to everything that exists, who has willed that "something" should exist and not "nothing" instead.

🔥 We Christians call this "Someone", who has created the universe out of nothing, God.

→ 2
Why did God create us?

🔥 And we say that God is the **CREATOR** of the world.

→ 44

Who created the world?

However, we must not imagine the Creator as someone who in the beginning made all things with a snap of his fingers and then sat back and rested. It was not only in the beginning that God spoke his great "Yes" to the world. He does so still, in every millisecond. Forever, until the end of the world, he continues to speak his great yes-world-I-will-that-you-exist.

> We are not some casual and meaningless product of evolution. Each of us is the result of a thought of God. Each of us is willed, each of us is loved, each of us is necessary.
>
> POPE BENEDICT XVI
> April 24, 2005

Without God's "Yes", which he speaks in this very second while you are reading these words, the universe with all its Milky Ways and solar systems would instantly sink into nothingness—just as though someone had switched off the projector and the film was over.

The end of the little gray brain cells

How can we actually know anything at all about God?

In order to know *the fact* of God's existence, our little gray brain cells are enough. To know that God must exist, one does not need much more than a logical mind. The idea of a world in which everything has a reason except for the world itself must strike any reasonable person as nonsense.

But of course we would like to know more about this mysterious being without whom **EVERYTHING** would be **NOTHING**.

Who is this God, then? What is his relationship toward what he has created? What is God himself like? Is God perhaps cold and cruel? Is he without feelings, like a machine? Or is he perhaps full of love?

Of himself, man can give no answer to these questions. Not even the greatest philosophers and thinkers can do so. Not Aristotle, not Plato, not Kant, not Hegel. And anyone who claims to be able to know what God himself is like is either nuts or a fraud.

What? So do we humans have *no chance* of knowing whether the ultimate cause of the universe is good or evil? Whether we can trust in the Creator of the world because he is good? Or whether we have been thrust into this world by a cruel tyrant, who simply toys with us, only to utterly annihilate us tomorrow or the day after?

But there is such a possibility. God could decide to communicate with us. We call this **REVELATION.** In what way could he do this? Perhaps like this:

🔥 He might write in giant letters of flame along the horizon: "I do exist. And actually I am nice. God."

→ 4

Can we know the existence of God by our reason?

→ 7

Why did God have to show himself in order for us to be able to know what he is like?

> 99 In His goodness and wisdom God chose to reveal Himself and to make known to us the hidden purpose of His will ... by which through Christ, the Word made flesh, man might in the Holy Spirt have access to the Father and come to share in the divine nature.
>
> Second Vatican Council, *Dei Verbum*

In many and various ways God spoke of old to our fathers by the prophets; but in these last days he has spoken to us by a Son, whom he appointed the heir of all things, through whom also he created the ages.

HEB 1:1–2

He might announce divine news bulletins, ringing out over the world in a voice of thunder: "Today I have decided ... etc.", or: "The next news bulletin from me will be on Wednesday. God."

Think for a moment about the word **REVELATION.** It's a bit like when you fall in love. You know nothing about the boy or girl of your dreams until you suddenly click and one of you says to the other, "Do you know, I've fallen totally in love with you!" You may have watched each other and had your eye on each other—or you may even have read books about men and women and the meaning of love. But you know nothing! What counts is the moment when the other person **REVEALS** himself to you. He has to open his heart and say those amazing words: "All this time I have longed for nothing else but your love!"

Actually, God has revealed (or shown) himself to mankind in many different ways—sometimes as mighty and powerful (in natural events or in the fate of entire nations), and sometimes as quiet and gentle, in the way God touches an individual human heart. The amazing thing is that God really wants to talk to you and to me as though we were the only people in the world—and the most important.

 → 20

How can we respond to God when he speaks to us?

If we have understood this and choose to listen to God's voice, then that is what we call faith.

God shows himself to me. I hear God's voice—and I respond:

 → 21

Faith—what is it?

"There you are, my Lord and my God. Thank you for seeing me and speaking within me. I **BELIEVE** in you. Lead me and guide me. Bless my life and the life of every person."

→ 22

How does one go about believing?

When a person recognizes the God who reveals himself, when he believes in him and responds to him in his heart, then that is what we call **PRAYER.**

A God who reveals himself, and a book like no other
God has to reveal himself so that we can understand

more about him. And that is exactly what HE does. The eternal, Almighty God, who is unfathomable to us men, actually did (and does) emerge from his silence. HE reveals himself. God even lays bare something of his innermost thoughts. He allows us to look into his very Heart—if one can speak of God in such terms. That is what happens in your life and in the lives of all those who listen in prayer to the voice of God and who seek and have sought for the footsteps of God in their lives. And we aren't starting from scratch in this.

The **BIBLE** is the book where you can read how God first showed himself in the history of the people of Israel, how he revealed himself little by little to mankind, until in Jesus he gave expression to the most profound truth about himself—that is to say, how immense his divine love is.

For long ages men had only vague notions about God or the gods. Entire nations imagined God to be a being to whom they even had to offer human sacrifices in order to gain his favor. Only in the life of the people of Israel does it become clear that God is no many-headed monster of whom they must live permanently in fear. The truth that there is only one God, that he is good and faithful to those who trust in him, has been revealed in the lives of many individual men and women—mothers, fathers, children, prophets, kings, and saints. Abraham encounters God beneath the starry sky, while Moses encounters him in the burning thorn bush. You know the stories.

All these experiences of God's presence were written down—in an unbelievably colorful and rich book. Pope Benedict XVI once compared the **BIBLE** to a garden, a bright and wonderfully beautiful garden in which the most profound insights about God appear like exquisite flowers. If we read the **BIBLE** and stay in touch with God as we do so, then "it is as if we were to find ourselves stolling in the garden of the Holy Spirit", the Pope said. "We talk to him and he talks to us."

 → 8
How does God reveal himself in the Old Testament?

 → 9
What does God show us about himself when he sends his Son to us?

→ Genesis 19;
→ Exodus 3

 → 16
What is the right way to read the Bible?

POOR EARTH, YOU ARE SICK

3 Why the World Is Broken

We would all love it if the earth were a paradise. But however hard politicians, philosophers, and teachers may try, they will simply not succeed in making people act humanely, in ending hunger, or abolishing sickness and even death.

→ 66
Was it part of God's plan for men to suffer and die?

3.1 The South Sea paradise

The philosopher Jean-Jacques Rousseau believed that man was by nature good and had only been ruined by civilization and by Christianity. Somewhere in the wilds of South America, or perhaps in the South Pacific, he thought, there must be "noble savages", who still lived in a kind of paradise because people hadn't filled their minds with all that nonsense about sin.

How did Rousseau picture such people?

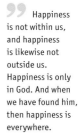

- The "noble savages" would live in perfect harmony with nature
- They would need no money
- They would be gentle and innocent
- They could not help but love each other
- They would not know what sin and crime were
- Lies would be unknown to them
- They would need no one to rule over them or judge them
- They would enjoy perfect health
- They would be naked and sexually unrestrained

Over 100 years after Rousseau, the painter Paul Gauguin also cherished this South Sea fantasy: "Free at last, without money worries, I would then love, sing, and die", he wrote in 1890 in a letter to his wife, Mette. In fact, Gauguin did eventually travel to the South Pacific and from there raved about it to his friends in Paris. There, "in the jungle, in the interior of the island", he wrote, he had indeed discovered the innocent, "noble savage". Money and worldly cares were unknown there. Instead, their lives consisted only of singing, dancing, and "free love".

99 Happiness is not within us, and happiness is likewise not outside us. Happiness is only in God. And when we have found him, then happiness is everywhere.

BLAISE PASCAL
(1588–1651, French mathematician and philosopher)

Puff!

The truth in fact was quite different. Gauguin was profoundly disillusioned. The bananas didn't simply fall off the trees for him, and he could neither fish nor hunt. As a result, he lived on expensive imported preserves. And as for the "noble savages", they suffered from all kinds of illnesses, fought a harsh struggle for survival, and had a strict moral code. The beautiful girls whom Gauguin wanted to paint were not allowed near him. Gauguin had to hire a girl to let him paint her.

Conclusion:
- Neither Jean-Jacques Rousseau
- nor Paul Gauguin
- nor anybody else …

… has ever yet found the "naturally good man". Rousseau himself was no exception. The philosopher, who saw himself as a great educator of humanity, never brought up a child himself. In fact, he had five children, but after they were born, he put all of them in an orphanage.

→ **Romans 7:15–25**

 ### "I don't do the good I want to do, but instead I do the bad things I don't want to do"

Of course, it is quite easy to make fun of Rousseau or Gauguin, but actually it would be better to show some honesty and humility and see the flaws in our own lives. Every one of us has some kind of fault or defect in our character. Some people see it sooner, others later. Sometimes we get mad at ourselves:

"I wanted to do it so well! But now I've gone and done the exact opposite. What a fool I am!"

Just imagine, even Saint Paul had the same experience. Read his words closely—it's quite an eye-opener!

3.3 **So will it always be that way?**

In thinking about this kind of experience, believers speak of "original sin" and its consequences. It's like this:

→ 69

Are we compelled to sin by original sin?

- We all seek what is good.
- But somehow we are under some kind of compulsion.
- It's as though someone is telling us to do the exact opposite.
- Again and again; again and again and again.
- Nothing seems to help—no good upbringing, no amount of persuasion, no psychology.

The world is broken. We no longer live in a paradise.

The Bible also speaks of paradise—of the paradise that is lost and of the paradise to which God longs to lead us home, namely, heaven. The Bible explains about original sin (and, with it, man's expulsion from paradise) in the story of the Fall of Adam and Eve.

→ Genesis 2:7–17;
→ Genesis 3

→ 68 *Original sin? What does the Fall of Adam and Eve have to do with us?*

Sin, in the proper sense, is a fault for which we are personally responsible. Hence the term "original sin" (inherited sin, inherited guilt) does not mean a personal sin but, rather, the unfortunate condition of mankind into which the human individual is born, even before he himself can sin by his own free decision. In the case of the Fall, said Pope Benedict XVI, we have to understand …

… that we all carry within us a drop of the poison of that way of thinking, illustrated by the images in the Book of Genesis. … The human being does not trust God. Tempted by the serpent, he harbors the suspicion that … God is a rival who curtails our freedom and that we will be fully human only when we have cast him aside … Man does not want to receive his existence and the fullness of his life from God. … And in doing so, he trusts in deceit rather than in truth and thereby sinks with his life into emptiness, into death. POPE BENEDICT XVI (December 8, 2005)

3.4 An engineer explains original sin

In a catechetical talk, Cardinal Schönborn of Vienna told how an engineer had once made it really clear to him just what is involved in *"inherited"* or *original* sin. He explains:

→ 70

How does God draw us out of the whirlpool of evil?

"One day an engineer (a good engineer) gave me the most beautiful definition of original sin that I have so far heard—or, shall we say, a very appealing and simple one. From his engineering experience, he knows that for every gadget you need an instruction manual. If I fail to follow the instructions in the manual, then I cannot complain if the piece of equipment doesn't work. This engineer put it to me that original sin, or, to put it more precisely, the first sin of our ancestors, was the refusal to follow the instruction manual. God has given us a human nature; we are creatures, and written within our crea-

turely nature, so to speak, are the correct instructions. If we then use ourselves differently, then we have no right to blame God if things do not work. Original sin is the refusal to accept our creaturely nature; it is the desire to be like God, but without God, the desire not to be told how by God but, rather, to do it ourselves. 'You will be like God.' "

 The key to paradise
Please, what is the way to paradise?

> We have lost paradise but gained heaven. Hence our gain is greater than our loss.
>
> SAINT JOHN CHRYSOSTOM

Not the way of Rousseau, who imagined a paradise for himself; and not the way of Gauguin, who painted one for himself ...

But only through Jesus, who reopened to us the closed gates of paradise by restoring our rightful connection to God the Father.

And it began with Jesus living in such a way that it was as if the brokenness had never existed ...

4

Jesus—More than a Mere Man

There is a true story about the Russian Czar Peter the Great (1672–1725). As a young man, Peter was exceptionally eager for knowledge. He wanted to learn everything he possibly could, so that one day, when he finally wore the Czar's crown, he would be able to modernize his backward country.

"In Russia we could build ships as ingeniously as the Dutch do!" he said to himself. For at that time the Dutch were the foremost shipbuilders in the world. And so the future Czar, under an assumed name, secretly slipped into a Dutch shipbuilder's yard and learned the trade of a ship's carpenter. Later, when Peter became the Czar, he very quickly got the Russians building splendid sailing ships, too ...

4.1 A great idea for a film

That God should have become man is a still more incredible story than that the Czar should have pretended for a few years to be a carpenter. God becoming man—that sounds like a fairy tale or an amusing idea for a film.

→ 72
What does the name "Jesus" mean?

In Hollywood someone could have written a fantasy film script along these lines:
A fictional "god" is getting bored in heaven, so he hits on the crazy idea of dressing up one day as a man. He comes down to earth, but ends up looking a bit silly, because this "god" doesn't really have any idea how things work down here. He gets into the craziest situations, but fortunately this "god" has all kinds of magical tricks and miracles he can work, so that he can beam himself out of even the worst situations once again. Things only get difficult when he meets a wonderful girl, falls eternally in love, and doesn't want to go back to heaven ever again ...

→ 73
Why is Jesus called "Christ"?

We'd no doubt have laughed, gulped down our Coke, gobbled up the popcorn, and forgotten the film again in a day or two.

4.2 Better than any film—the thoughts of God

So what did God really do with his poor, broken, sin-damaged creation? Let's first of all say what he didn't do:

- He did not simply leave us floating around in space, forgotten.
- He did not stop loving us and never ceased to be faithful to us.
- He did not send down a great punishment on a world in which hatred, greed, and envy seem to rule, where people torment one another, let others starve, rob others of their opportunities and their just wages—a world in which the children are no better than their parents.
- He did not send down the "death penalty" on us for our sins.

What did God do instead?

- He saw our sorrows and our tears because we have to die.
- God decided to share everything with us except sin.
- In Jesus of Nazareth, God took on our human nature. He was the son of a Jewish maiden, Mary, and was born over two thousand years ago in Bethlehem.

4.3 God—a baby?

Can you imagine it: GOD—a crying baby, a baby nursed at his mother's breast, a baby in diapers? A child, tearing down the road, skinning his knees, and running, crying, to his mother? A young man, proud of his growing strength and understanding, sharing his joys and sorrows with his friends, both boys and girls, experiencing temptations just as we do ... and yet coming to understand ever more deeply that despite everything he is not of this world because, in a profound and unique way, he is still united with his Father in heaven. Can you imagine that?

As I live, says the Lord GOD, I have no pleasure in the death of the wicked, but that the wicked turn from his way and live.

EZEK 33:11

→ 76

Why did God become man in Jesus?

→ John 3:16

→ 79

Did Jesus have a soul, a mind, and a body, just as we do?

If you find it difficult, you are not alone. Many of the Christians of the first century had actually known and seen Jesus, first hand.

- They saw a real human being, with whom they could laugh, cry, eat, drink, sing, have fun.
- But they also saw a Jesus who could work miracles and even raise the dead to life. They sensed a superhuman power in his words—and, above all, they witnessed the fact that death had no power over him. Around the year 30 A.D., under Pontius Pilate, Jesus was brutally executed on the Cross, and his death was unequivocally witnessed. But after his death, he was seen alive by many people, even, on one occasion, by "more than five hundred brethren at one time" (1 Cor 15:6).

→ 77

What does it mean to say that Jesus Christ is at the same time true God and true man?

You can imagine how much discussion there was about that in the early Church, until the year 451, in the Council of Chalcedon (which is today a suburb of Istanbul, Turkey) they finally agreed on the formula "both true God and true man".

So human and yet so divine—the story of Lazarus

Many people who saw Jesus above all as God took exception to the idea that Jesus obviously had a genuine personal friend in Lazarus. If he were God, they said, then surely he could not have had individual, personal friendships. And yet he did. The Bible does not tell us in detail about their friendship, but clearly they were often together and enjoyed each other's company, whether walking in the hills or sitting together talking by the shores of the Sea of Galilee. Now Saint John's Gospel tells about one occasion when apparently Jesus definitely arrived too late to see his friend who had died.

→ **John 11:1–46**

Ask yourself: What is so divine and yet so human about Jesus?

No suffering that God does not know about

Just imagine that someone turns round to you and says:

"Get away from me with your God! I don't need a God who sits in heaven in happiness. I've been through things that no God can have experienced! There was no God in the kind of hell I've been through."

And then maybe he says to you:

"I've been through this and that sickness ... I was in mortal peril ... I was ostracized and bullied ... I was betrayed by my friends ... I was unjustly condemned ... I was beaten up and tortured ..."

What can you say in reply? Maybe this:

→ Heb 4:14–16

"I don't know what kind of God you're talking about. My God was wounded and in fear of his life; he was blasphemed against and persecuted; he was betrayed by one of his best friends; he was unjustly condemned and tortured to death. He went through what no god had been through before: in fact he went through hell. Take my God, if yours is not enough for you!"

→ 60

Why is Jesus the greatest example in the world?

When it comes to Jesus, opinions differ sharply. Was he truly God, acting with the power of God, or was he a con man, a false prophet, a blasphemer, and a criminal? Those who hated him could see only that he was putting himself in the position of God—presuming to forgive sins and relativize the law on the Sabbath ... Surely these were crimes worthy of death?

That's how it looked on the outside. But why ...

 → 96

Why was a man of peace like Jesus condemned to death on a Cross?

- Why did Jesus come to such a chaotic place as Jerusalem, knowing that he would die there?
- Why did he submit to the judgment?
- Why did he not call on his followers to fight back?
- Why did heaven not react?

There is only one possible answer to this:

Jesus knowingly accepted death. He wanted to do the Father's will.

→ 94

Did Jesus know that he would die when he entered Jerusalem?

We are always being told: Jesus did this for love of us. Or else: He did it to redeem us, through his suffering. But what does that really mean?

→ 98

Did God will the death of his only Son?

5.1 What did Jesus actually suffer?

Perhaps you've seen the film *The Passion of Christ*, by Mel Gibson? Some people say it's a bad film that relies only on brutal effects. And that the film is nothing but a revolting orgy of sadism, blood, and violence.

Others reply: What do you expect? That's more or less exactly what happened when Jesus was put to death.

Crucifixion was surely one of the most horrific forms of execution of ancient times. No Roman was allowed to be crucified. In fact, for the most part, it was the punishment reserved for

 → 101

Why did Jesus
have to redeem us
on the Cross, of all
places?

slaves who had run away. Jesus was nailed to the Cross. But not only that: they mocked him and tortured him first. Take a look at the picture on the next page, which is one of many ancient portrayals of the "instruments of the Passion" of Christ that you will find in old medieval churches (this one is in the Wendelin Chapel in the village of Bremenried, in Bavaria, Germany). It shows:

- the **chalice of suffering**, which reminds us of the blood that "is poured out for you" (Lk 22:20).
- the **sponge soaked in vinegar**, on the end of a stick, that was given to Jesus to quench his thirst.
- the **nails** that were hammered through the hands of Jesus.
- the **crown of thorns** that was used to mock Jesus.
- the **clothes** Jesus wore that were torn from his body, so that he would die naked and without dignity.

- The **jug of water** that Pilate used to wash his hands in pretended innocence, after handing over Jesus to be crucified.
- The **dice** that were used by the soldiers to cast lots for Jesus' robe.
- The **pincers** used to remove the nails from the body of Jesus.
- The **lance** with which the heart of Jesus was pierced.
- The **scourge** that was used to beat Jesus to the point of physical collapse while he was chained to a pillar.
- The **ladders** that were used to take the body of Jesus down from the Cross.

These "instruments of the Passion" naturally caused Jesus terrible sufferings. But if Jesus had "only" suffered from these things, what would have distinguished him from, say, each of the 6,000 slaves who were crucified after the failed Spartacus rebellion (73–71 B.C.) along the miles of the Appian Way, outside the gates of Rome? What would distinguish his suffering and anguish from that of the Jewish children in the gas chambers of Auschwitz?

There is one crucial difference that distinguishes the sufferings of Jesus from that of the millions upon millions of other human beings:

The man who was nailed to the Cross here was not merely a man. The man who died here was Love itself—the Son of God made man.

So what did Jesus actually suffer? He suffered all the hatred, all the evil, all the sins, all the crimes, all the unlove that have ever darkened this earth.

He also suffered because of you and me.

 → 102

Why are we, too, supposed to accept suffering in our lives and thus "take up our cross" and thereby follow Jesus?

5.2 The killer punch

In boxing, they sometimes speak of a boxer having a "killer punch"—implying that it is so powerful it can kill a man. With one single movement, he can deliver a blow of such force that his opponent is simply annihilated by it. Naturally, it is fair enough for a boxer to want to deliver a knockout punch to his opponent, but it has indeed happened, unfortunately, that boxers have been killed in the ring by a fatal punch from their opponent.

> The snow melts in the spring. It can never destroy the rays of the sun. No more can evil destroy love.
>
> RICHARD WURMBRAND
> (1909–2001, Christian minister)

When God became man in order to prove his boundless love for us, then **EVIL**, too, prepared to deliver a deadly blow. As it says in an ancient Easter hymn, "Death with life contended: combat strangely ended!…"

It was as though all the wickedness and all the evil in the world had gathered together during these dark days of April in A.D. 30 in Jerusalem in order to wipe out **LOVE** itself, to wipe out **JESUS.** The resulting situation was one that the devil himself might well have devised.

A situation of hatred, lies, and false testimony, of cold, calculating cynicism, of power struggles, brutality, torture, cowardice, lethargy, betrayal, silence.

As we have said, it was as though all the evil in the world had gathered together to deliver the "killer punch" to love.

And what did Jesus do?

He stood there and took it. He did not hit back. He did not defend himself. He stood there, silent, in front of Pilate. He took the Cross on his shoulders. He let the whole power of evil and sin vent its rage on him. He died, so as to make a new beginning for the world.

 → 99

What happened at the Last Supper?

He gave his life—for you and me as well.

 → 100

On the Mount of Olives on the night before his death, did Jesus really experience fear of death?

5.3 What did Jesus himself mean by his death?

We can speculate a lot about the death of Jesus, but it is best to stick to the Bible. Jesus himself did in fact speak about the meaning of his death. The evangelists have written this down—not necessarily word for word, but certainly an essentially trustworthy account. We need to read these sacred texts again and again (and ask the Holy Spirit to help us in our understanding) so that we can understand each time more deeply what is meant by them.

→ John 13:1–15

5.4 A female volleyball player, a Franciscan monk, and a man who refused to bow to Hitler

What do people actually achieve when they die for other people? Wouldn't it have been better to have stayed alive? Before we go on to talk about Jesus, it would be worth taking a look at three ordinary people who did precisely this.

What?
My life for yours?!
A couple of examples

Agata Mróz (1982–2008), a player on the Polish national volleyball team, was not only as beautiful as any top model and a superb sportswoman as well (European champions twice over), she was at the same time a remarkable Christian woman. Agata died of cancer in June 2008. Right up to the birth of her daughter in April of the same year, she refused any form of treatment that might damage her unborn child. She died at the age of 27—and saved the life of her child. Shortly before she died, she said, *"I do not regret my decision. If I had to choose again, I would do exactly the same thing. I am happy, and I die fulfilled and at peace."*

It was the year 1943, in Auschwitz, one of the Nazis' most notorious death camps. One of the

prisoners was quite famous, a brilliant man who was well known all over Poland. His name was Maximilian Kolbe, a Franciscan priest. At the age of only 33, he had founded an enormous monastery complex with its own publishing house, printing press, workshops, and radio station, in addition to the monastery itself and an attached grammar school. In 1939 he was seized by the Nazis and finally brought to Auschwitz. It was here that something extraordinary happened. One day Maximilian saw a man who was about to be executed. His name was Franciszek Gajowniczek, and Maximilian knew that he had a wife and children. Spontaneously, he stepped forward and said to the SS soldiers, *"Let this man live. Take my life instead of his."* The Nazis accepted his offer, and Maximilian Kolbe was dragged off and thrown into an underground prison cell, where he was left to starve to death with a group of other prisoners. For the next

two weeks, people passing by his cell could hear him praying and singing. He was the last man to die, finally killed by lethal injection. When Maximilian Kolbe was canonized in 1982, Franciszek Gajowniczek stood on Saint Peter's Square and could not hold back his tears.

The Austrian Pallottine priest Franz Reinisch had very quickly realized that Hitler was a criminal. *"As a Christian ... I can never swear an oath of loyalty to a man like Hitler,"* he said. *"There have to be people willing to protest against the abuse of authority, and I feel that I am called to make this protest."* He knew that sooner  or later he was going to be called up and would be required to swear the oath of loyalty to Hitler. Friends and superiors tried to dissuade him, with good arguments and even orders, from taking such a courageous step; but in vain. When he was drafted, in April 1942, he plainly stated, right at the barrack gates, that he would not swear the oath of loyalty to Hitler. He was arrested at once. On August 21, 1942, he was executed. At midnight he made his last confession; at 1 A.M., he received Holy Communion. At 3 A.M., he gave away his last remaining possessions—his crucifix, his rosary beads, his few books, and his farewell letter. At 3:30 A.M., they removed his shoes and socks, tied his hands behind his back, and took him into the cellar room next to the execution cell. At 5:03 A.M., Franz Reinisch was beheaded.

Agata Mróz died for the sake of her child.

Maximilian Kolbe died for the sake of Franciszek Gajowniczek.

Franz Reinisch died for the sake of all those who did not have the courage to stand up to Hitler themselves.

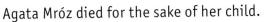

 → 87

Why did Jesus allow John to baptize him, although he was without sin?

5.5 In place of others—a mystery

We need others to act in our place when we ourselves cannot be there:

🔥 No one could have saved the life of Agata's child but Agata Mróz herself.

🔥 There was no one else there with the strength to save Francizek Gajowniczek from the starvation bunker except Maximilian Kolbe.

🔥 Nobody except Franz Reinisch had received the God-given insight to realize that it was better to die than to swear loyalty to a criminal.

→ 70

How does God draw us out of the whirlpool of evil?

So why did **Jesus** die, then? Because there was no one else who could do in his place what he himself did for us.

🔥 We belong to a world that has fallen away from God and that continues to distance itself from him at breakneck speed.

🔥 We can't pull ourselves up by our own bootstraps. We need God to rescue us. We need someone to save us and bring us home.

🔥 In Jesus, God came down to us in his fullness. Into our world of original sin. Into all the misery of our alienation from God. Into the darkness of our sins. Into our sorrows, our suffering, our weeping, our desperation, our inevitable dying. Even into the concentration camps and the gas chambers.

→ **Philippians 2:6–8**

🔥 We can go on indefinitely running away from God. But even when we have reached rock bottom, there is still someone there for us—Jesus Christ.

🔥 Even in the valley of death, LOVE still waits for us.

→ 76

Why did God become man in Jesus?

🔥 When Agata Mróz, St. Maximilian Kolbe, and Fr. Franz Reinisch arrived in the valley of death, they were welcomed by Jesus, who took them up with him into joy, into the great Feast of Life, which is eternal communion with God.

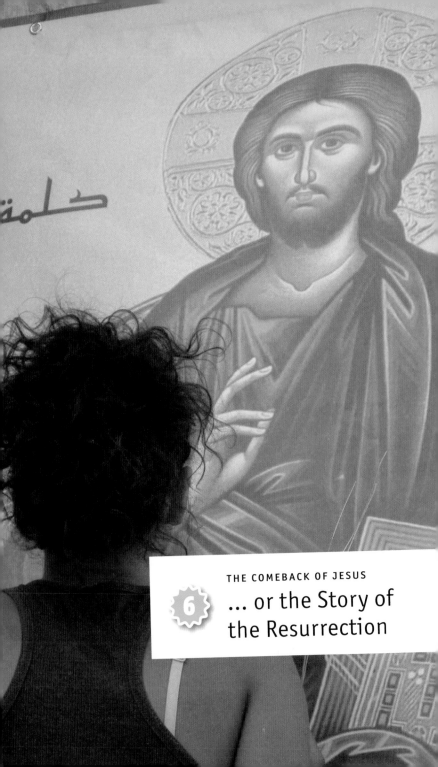

THE COMEBACK OF JESUS

6

... or the Story of the Resurrection

There's an old saying in the boxing world: "They never come back." Meaning those great champions who once won every battle. One day a new kid comes along and knocks the old champion out of the ring. The old guy finds it hard to take; he cannot rest. He tries to make a comeback, to show everyone just one more time he's still the best. Usually, it ends in disaster, and the former champion takes a heavy beating. Humiliated, he creeps out of the ring. A boxing legend is finally destroyed.

6.1 The destruction of a legend

What had happened? Jesus was the great star of his times. Like a comet, he had soared to the heights and had drawn others behind him like a comet's tail—friends, disciples, apostles, the curious, the sensation seekers, the political activists ... And indeed, there was something to get excited about:

- Jesus must have been a gifted speaker who knew how to captivate the crowds.

 → 90

Did Jesus work miracles, or are they just pious tales?

- With Jesus, people must have been expecting a miracle every time. The Bible tells us of blind men who could suddenly see, of cripples who could walk again, of the deaf who could now hear, of lepers suddenly healed of their putrid wounds and horrible scars. Jesus even raised the dead to life again (and they really were dead, not just pretending; for example, in the case of Lazarus, Martha says to Jesus: "Lord, by this time there will be an odor, for he has been dead four days").

 → John 11:39

- Jesus encouraged people to go with him to Jerusalem—and in a politically delicate situation. The country was occupied by the Romans. Was this the beginning of a bloody revolt against the hated occupiers? Many Jews were hoping for a liberator, and for a long time now the rumor had been circulating that a "Messiah", sent by God, would come and sweep the Romans out of the country by force.

 → 73

Why is Jesus called "Christ"?

→ 95

Why did Jesus choose the date of the Jewish feast of Passover for his death and Resurrection?

And then came those decisive days in Jerusalem. The authorities in Jerusalem needed no spies and no Secret Service to tell them that this dangerous man Jesus was in the city. And on the feast of Passover, of all times, when Jewish pilgrims from every nation—including Egypt, for example—came thronging by the thousands into the Holy City. On the day of this great feast, the skies would be darkened by the thick smoke from the burnt offerings of 18,000 lambs. Was the Prophet from Nazareth going to appear and set the city ablaze in a quite different way? There were many who hoped so. Others were taking counsel together, to see how they could put a stop to Jesus once and for all. The leaders in Jerusalem knew very well that there was no sense in provoking the overwhelming occupying forces of the world power, Rome—it would simply end in a bloodbath.

He was oppressed, and he was afflicted, yet he opened not his mouth; like a lamb that is led to the slaughter, and like a sheep that before its shearers is silent, so he opened not his mouth.

Is 53:7

But with Jesus things are quite different:

Like a defenseless lamb, he lets himself be led to the slaughter.
Saint Peter has to put his drawn sword back in its scabbard.
Hauled before the tribunal, Jesus remains silent.
He submits to everything.

If Jesus was once the invincible champion to his disciples, then Golgotha was the destruction of a legend.

→ Matthew 26:69–75

6.2 Let's get out of here!

The arrest and condemnation of Jesus, his apparent helplessness and his death on the Cross as a criminal must have been such a crushing disappointment to his followers that even Peter, who was one of the very closest friends of Jesus, nevertheless betrayed him in an incomprehensible manner, saying: "I do not know the man!" (Mt 26:74) when people asked him about his hero.

When Jesus was finally condemned and executed, all the rest of his disciples likewise took to their heels. They simply ran away, each one in a different direction. What was a fisherman going to say to his friends? "Hi folks, I'm back again! When are we going out?"

What do you do in a situation like that, as a devoted follower of someone who has ignominiously disappeared from the scene? You lie low. You hide away for a while. You don't want to be reminded about the past any more.

But how can it be, then,

that from this story of a "loser" the greatest religious community in the world has developed? Today almost two billion people—a quarter of the world's population—declare themselves Christians.

6.3 A world religion is born

Within just 30 short years after Jesus' death, the new religion of Christianity had reached almost the entire ancient Roman world, including its capital. Starting out from tiny communities (house churches), an unprecedented triumphal march began that reminds one of the parable of the mustard seed. A wave of joy swept across country after country. Many great and highly respected figures were also converted and received baptism alongside the slaves. The young Christian communities were frequently persecuted; indeed, there were attempts to exterminate them. Many Christians were thrown to the lions in the ancient stadiums. But the people of Jesus would rather have died than betray their faith.

And so, through Jesus, there was what must have been an incredible new beginning. Within the briefest space of time, something happened that gripped these disillusioned farmers and fishermen and transformed them, something that once again called people away from their fields and out of their boats and turned them, in the twinkling of an eye, into fervent missionaries and messengers of the faith.

So what on earth was it …

that made these simple men and women from the province of Galilee into such compelling witnesses to their faith and led, within three centuries, to the conversion of Greek philoso-

In the Cross is salvation; in the Cross is life; in the Cross is protection against our enemies.

THOMAS À KEMPIS (1379/1380–1471), *The Imitation of Christ*

→ **Matthew 13:31–32**

If the Tiber rises too high for the walls, or the Nile too low for the fields, if the heavens do not open, or the earth does; if there is famine, if there is plague, instantly the howl is, The Christians to the lion!

TERTULLIAN, (Apologeticum) ca. 197 A.D.

phers and Roman emperors? As to what caused this sensational new start, based on Jesus, there are many different views.

Some possible answers:

→ John 11:27

→ 107

Through his Resurrection, did Jesus return to the physical, corporeal state that he had during his earthly life?

1 The story of Jesus' Resurrection is true—and it is the one and only driving force behind the greatest comeback in world history. He who was truly dead came back to life. Yet he was now quite different; he passed through closed doors and so no longer shared our ordinary mortal life. But he was undoubtedly alive—and forever. His disciples experienced this for themselves, because the risen Jesus showed himself to them in such a living form that Thomas was even able to put his hand into the wound in Jesus' side. It was their living Lord himself who roused the disciples, for the second time, from their normal world. This was how the earliest Christian community was formed. The mysterious key to their missionary success was the **RISEN CHRIST** himself, living mysteriously in their midst. And the young Church now had yet another incredible message to offer: Whoever stays faithful to Jesus has eternal life "even if he dies".

→ John 20:24–29

→ 103

Was Jesus really dead? Maybe he was able to rise again because he only appeared to have suffered death?

This is the conviction of the Church. And she has a wealth of good reasons for it.

2 Some people say that Jesus only *seemed* to be dead. He was freed from the tomb—and then Jesus reorganized his group and made his comeback as the "Christian world religion". Later he died in peace and now lies buried in some unknown place.

Highly improbable! Not only was he crucified, he also had a spear thrust through his heart.

3 Some people said Jesus was dead and he never rose. His disciples removed his body from the tomb. The legend of the 'empty tomb' then gave rise to the belief in his resurrection. The disciples made use of this pretty fairy tale in order to help them better proclaim the message of Jesus.

So the disciples of Jesus were grave robbers and liars then? No. There were too many witnesses who saw him for that to be true.

4 Some people say there was a comeback—of sorts—even though Jesus was dead, stayed dead, and is still dead. So dead, in fact, that we may one day find his bones and be able to determine his DNA. Jesus' comeback consisted merely in the fact that his "cause" went on. It was not Jesus but only the profound wisdom of his words that "lived on" and continues to "live on".

This is a mistaken interpretation that one finds here and there even within the Church. It is a view usually taken by people who assume all miracles to be nonsense. So how do they account for the amazingly rapid spread of Christianity, then? As a sort of "flash mob" of God, perhaps? With more and more people yelling "Hallelujah, Jesus lives!"?

6.4 A twinge of doubt—a "flash mob" of God?

Have you ever witnessed a real flash mob? There is a really cool one on the internet. It's only a few days before Christmas, and we find ourselves inside a vast shopping mall. People are rushing to and fro with shopping bags; some are sitting wearily at tables, drinking a latte or a Coke. Everyone looks a bit glum. Suddenly, someone stands up, climbs onto a chair and sings out at the top of his voice: "Hallelujah, hallelujah...". You've surely heard of the Hallelujah Chorus from Handel's *Messiah*? Heads turn everywhere. Has the man lost his mind? Then a few seconds later, from another corner, another voice joins in. What? Two of them now? Are they both crazy? But it sounds great. Then a third voice. Then someone else puts his coffee cup down and stands up to sing, heartily. Within a couple of minutes, half the shopping center is singing. People

If Christ has not been raised, your faith is futile and you are still in your sins.

1 Cor 15:17

" The event of the death and resurrection of Christ [is] the heart of Christianity, the fulcrum and mainstay of our faith, the firm lever of our certainties, the strong wind that sweeps away all fear and indecision, all doubt and human calculation.

POPE BENEDICT XVI, May 11, 2010

laugh, shake their heads; and soon even the slowest of them have realized: this is no accident. This is a brilliant choir that has cleverly staged a flash mob event. In other words, they have arranged it all in advance. The members of the choir simply pretended they were just casual customers in the shopping mall and had nothing to do with one another. But in reality, they had been practicing for months for the flash mob event, even though it appeared to be totally spontaneous.

Might not the story of the Resurrection really have been like that?

After the disciples had been scattered to the four winds for awhile, they thought better of it, because they simply could not forget Jesus. So they could have said to themselves: *Even if Jesus has failed, yet we still have his teachings—and if we follow them, then Jesus will still "live on", in a manner of speaking. From this arose the original community, who were "one heart and one soul". Within this community, all kinds of people testified that "Jesus" was "living" in their souls. In order to convince the Jews and Greeks of this "life", Paul and the evangelists invented the symbolic story, intended for teaching, of the empty tomb and the resurrection of Jesus from the dead.*

So, what are we to make of this idea? Resurrection merely as a "symbol", a sort of collusion within the Church? ("We're going to call it 'Resurrection' now!") If the true story of Christianity had indeed been merely a sort of "flash mob" event, organized by some of the disciples, one could only urge everyone to leave the Church at once and on no account agree to be confirmed. For then the central event of the Christian faith would be an invention and the apostles would be the ones considered con men who had pulled the wool over the eyes of the ancient world.

→ 104

Can you be a Christian without believing in the Resurrection of Christ?

At Easter the Church sings:

Christ is risen. He is truly risen. Alleluia!

And this is not simply the song of some prearranged flash mob, all singing alleluia together. The Church believes what she sings.

6.5 Scenes from a comeback

Why was the early Church so sure about the Resurrection of Jesus that no one would ever have dreamed of considering it a fake?

→ 105

How did the disciples come to believe that Jesus is risen?

Let us look at the earliest account that exists of the Resurrection of Jesus. It dates from around the year 55—so that's roughly 25 years after the death of Jesus—and it was written by Saint Paul. Paul was not himself an eyewitness of the events that took place at that time in Jerusalem, but he relied on the testimony of those who had been eyewitnesses. And if you count up those mentioned in his account, there may well have been as many as 520 people to whom Jesus appeared, or even more. Here they are:

- "to Cephas" (the Rock—by which he means Peter, the head of the Apostles)
- "to more than five hundred brethren at one time"
- "then to James"
- "… then to all the apostles"
- "last of all … to me." ("as to one untimely born …". Some even translate this as "abnormally born").

→ 1 Corinthians 15:3–9

Read this important passage from the First Letter of Paul to the Corinthians!

Why did Saint Paul describe himself as "abnormally born", and how could he say that the risen Christ also appeared to him, when he only later joined the young Christian community? To answer this we need to know the story of Paul, whose Jewish name was in fact Saul.

The early Christian community feared this name more than any other. For Saul was a militant persecutor of the Christians and had their blood on his hands. "Saul", the Acts of the Apostles tell us, was "still breathing threats and murder against the disciples of the Lord" (Acts 9:1). He was the man at whose feet the men laid their clothes when they stoned to death Saint Stephen, the first Christian martyr. And we are told that "Saul was consenting to his death" (Acts 8:1).

So now do you see why Paul describes himself as "abnormally born"? He had a pretty bad track record. Christ had to throw him from his horse and blind him in order to show him:

→ Acts 9:1–5

I exist, and you are persecuting the wrong people!
I am risen, and I live!

It was certainly a difficult "birth" that brought Paul into a new life.

→ Acts 9

You absolutely must read the thrilling account of Saint Paul in the Acts of the Apostles!

What a story it is! Jesus has chosen a man who denied him (Peter) and a man who persecuted the Christians (Paul) to help him establish his Church.

→ 106

Are there proofs for the Resurrection of Jesus?

In order to do so, he had to show himself to both of them in an absolutely unequivocal way as the RISEN and living LORD. So Paul, too, was entitled to describe himself as a "witness to the Resurrection".

That is the truth about Jesus' comeback.

6.6 And what does Jesus' comeback have to do with us?

Think for a moment about someone, perhaps one of your relatives, whom you knew and who has since died. Maybe an uncle or aunt, a grandfather or grandmother, or perhaps even a parent or one of your brothers or sisters?

(Thus says the Lord): "Can a woman forget her sucking child, that she should have no compassion on the son of her womb? Even these may forget, yet I will not forget you."

Is 49:15

- Do you believe that this dear person is totally gone forever? As though he had never existed?
- Do you believe that a good God could ever forget him?
- Can you imagine this person having a new life—in a new reality with God?

Many people cherish the hope that God does not simply wipe us away from the face of the earth.

That this is true ...

That, although we die, we will yet find new life ...

... is something we know ever since Jesus died and rose again. Jesus tells Martha, who was unwilling to believe that Lazarus could have new life through Jesus: *"I am the resurrection and the life; he who believes in me, though he die, yet shall he live, and whoever lives and believes in me shall never die."*

→ 108

What changed in the world as a result of the Resurrection?

→ John 11:25

And he goes on to ask her: "Do you believe this?"
This is a question that every Christian must answer:

Do you believe Jesus when he says this? —

DAMASCUS

FEEL THE SPIRIT!

7 In Search of the Holy Spirit

Confirmation means that the Holy Spirit comes down upon us. No doubt the word "spirit" is familiar enough to you. The word might make us think of ghosts in a haunted castle or the kind of alcoholic spirit you find in bottles (even if it's not always a good idea to drink it). Or again you might think of famous athletes or explorers who show an undaunted spirit of courage or determination. In the Church, we speak of the Holy Spirit and recall what happened at Pentecost, when he came down upon the apostles in "tongues as of fire". We need to search, or research, a little more deeply in order to understand better what (or, rather, who) the Holy Spirit really is.

→ Acts 2:1–5

7.1 The most sensible religion in the world

The people of Israel were rightly proud of the fact that theirs was, so to speak, the most sensible religion in the world. Other nations still imagined a different god behind every thunderclap. The ancient Greeks—whom we normally think of as world champions in thinking—still had, even at the time of Jesus, a heaven teeming with different gods. But the Jews knew that there could only be one God—Yahweh. They were monotheists—in other words, "one-God believers".

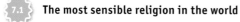

I am the LORD your God, who brought you out of the land of Egypt, out of the house of bondage. You shall have no other gods before me.

Ex 20:2–3; the First Commandment.

7.2 One, two, or three? Or what?

Then when Jesus came, things suddenly became complicated. His fellow Jews could well understand that Jesus would address the Lord in heaven as **FATHER.** This was clearly monotheistic. But then Jesus did things that only God can do—such as forgive sins and be the final authority for understanding the Law of Moses. What? Are there supposed to be two gods, now, after all? The **FATHER** and the **SON**? For many of the Jews, this was not merely a sliding back into primitive religion; it was so intolerable to them that they even wanted Jesus to be nailed to the Cross for it.

→ 35

Do we believe in one God or in three Gods?

But things were about to get even more extreme. When Jesus said farewell to his disciples, he promised them "another Counselor", the **HOLY SPIRIT.** At Pentecost, the disciples

→ John 14:16

understood what Jesus had meant by that, when the **HOLY SPIRIT** was poured out upon them.

What does it mean to say: I believe in the Holy Spirit?

→ 113

The disciples experienced a deep sense of security and joy in their faith and also received wonderful gifts **(CHARISMS)**. Suddenly, they were able to prophesy, heal people, work miracles. Ever since this time Christians have prayed to the **FATHER**, to the **SON**, and to the **HOLY SPIRIT**. And they also baptize "in the name of the Father, and of the Son, and of the Holy Spirit". So does that mean we're now talking about three gods?

→ John 20:19–22
→ Acts 2:1–4

What happened on Pentecost?

→ 118

No. Christians are not polytheists (people who believe in many gods). After long wrestling with this problem, the early Church finally came up with the formula: "One God in three Persons". We call this the **TRINITY**. There is in fact only one God. But, through Jesus, the Church has learned that within the deepest reality of this one God there is a community, an exchange, mutual love—between three distinct Persons.

7.3 The great Unknown

Many people say: I can understand Jesus, the *Son*. I can pray to the *Father*. But the *Holy Spirit* is still a stranger to me.

There is a very simple key to the Holy Spirit:

Who is the "Holy Spirit"?

→ 38

🜂 Think for a moment about the beginning. The Holy Spirit is the Spirit of God, the Power that filled Jesus; the Love that existed between Jesus and the Father; the Power by which Jesus healed others.

Under what names and signs does the Holy Spirit appear?

→ 115

🜂 When Jesus let himself be baptized in the River Jordan, something came down upon him from above, in the form of a dove. We might say today that God the Father sent him some kind thoughts or a kind of divine energy. But that does not really help. Kind thoughts are simply air; they come and go. Energy evaporates.

- Jesus did not receive any idea, nor was he charged with some kind of anonymous energy, like a battery. In the baptism of Jesus, his relationship with the Father was made visible.

- The Holy Spirit is the Love of God in person. That means we can speak to Love as to a close friend. It means that Love sees and hears. That Love himself answers us.

- Jesus gave us his Love, his Holy Spirit, as a gift. That means that what he gave us was not any kind of "novel ideas" copyrighted by Jesus; rather, he gave us his own Spirit as a living and real Person, who acts, to whom we can speak; who hears, answers, leads us, guides us; to whom we can pray, and so on.

- The Holy Spirit is with us, just as Jesus was with his disciples. He is just as close; just as accessible; just as attentive; just as healing; just as capable of the miraculous.

- This is what we must understand when we say that the Holy Spirit (of Jesus) lives in the Church and guides her. He lives in every single baptized Christian who has opened himself to the reality of God.

→ 114

What role does the Holy Spirit play in the life of Jesus?

Jesus is with his Father. But through the Holy Spirit we may experience him as essentially close to us as if he were still walking through the grainfields in Galilee or talking to us on the shores of Lake Gennesaret.

7.4 The Holy Spirit and your heart— Pentecost for you and me as well

At any big event or celebration today you can buy those shiny, heart-shaped balloons. All over the world the heart shape is the sign of love. Heart = Love!

Well, okay ... Heart = Love? Sure, it would be nice if every human heart were filled with this one sentiment of LOVE. That would be a real revolution, if every person approached others with heartfelt joy and deep, inner respect and affection!

But isn't there something in the Bible about all the evil things that come out of the heart of man? Jesus told us so himself.

→ Mark 7:21–22

TRY THIS EXPERIMENT:

Sit by yourself, all alone in your room, for five minutes—without your mobile phone, your laptop, your iPod ... Can you do it? Many people can't even hold out for three minutes. For there is so much going on within our hearts:

- There is a restlessness that rises within us, or sometimes an inexplicable sadness.
- Sometimes feelings of hatred and anger well up.
- Often we are gripped by a craving for things that aren't ours.
- Frequently there are feelings of envy within us toward other people whom we imagine to be better, smarter, better looking, more successful, more popular than we are.
- Occasionally we may feel as though our heart is one dark swamp of poisonous and troubled emotions.

Some people describe their feelings with words like: "I'm searching for a deep joy, but I can't find it." "There is an insatiable longing within me, like a great, deep chasm that nothing will fill." "I can't find peace within myself!"

 Why nothing seems to satisfy my heart

You don't need to be troubled by the fact that your heart is so big, so full of longing, so restless.

> You have made us for yourself, O God, and our heart is restless until it rests in you.
>
> SAINT AUGUSTINE OF HIPPO

God has created our heart in such a way that it is satisfied with nothing except God.

Let the great inner emptiness be there within you. It is there so that God can find a space to dwell within you. God wants us to be happy. He wants to fill us, right down to the last fiber of our being—not with some kind of anonymous "energy", but with himself. God never gives less than himself. He wants us to have joy without end. That is the reason he has made our heart so immeasurably wide and uninhabitable until it becomes the dwelling of his own Holy Spirit.

 → 338

What is grace?

And what will be dwelling in you then—instead of hatred, envy, ill will, fear, and greed? Love—nothing else but the Holy Spirit.

→ 1 John 4:16
→ 1 Corinthians 3:10

If it were otherwise, then even an unhappy-looking Russian oil billionaire would be the happiest man in the world. Having already built beautiful villas on all the most beautiful beaches of the earth, and with garages crammed full of all the most expensive luxury automobiles, like Rolls-Royces and Ferraris, in addition to all the light aircraft, helicopters, and luxury yachts in the Pacific, he decided to buy himself a soccer club as well. There is no knowing whether he was truly any happier as a result.

But even the most ordinary person, if he opens his heart to the Holy Spirit of God, can immediately find peace and joy—because Love himself comes to him and makes his home within him.

 → 120

What does the Holy Spirit do in my life?

7.6 Make me beautiful within

Have you ever been to Taizé, France? If not, then you should definitely go sometime. Taizé is really cool. Many people have found a deep faith in God there. In the summer months in particular, thousands of young people come there from all over the world. They camp in the fields or sleep in huts. In Taizé there are around 100 monks, most of them young. You can talk to them and take part in workshops. But the most beautiful thing of all is the prayer. Three times a day a bell rings out, and everyone—truly everyone—makes his way to the church. Even the most unlikely types, people you would never expect to find in any religious service! But then what an unusual church it is! First of all, there are no benches. You sit on the floor. And then there is no tinkling of a sacristy bell to begin the worship. Instead, the white-robed monks simply file in, one after another, and sit down in silence on the floor, among all the young people.

And suddenly, in the midst of the silence, you hear a single voice, singing "Veni, Sancte Spiritus!" It is sung very quietly. It means "Come, Holy Spirit!" Now other voices join in, also singing "Veni, Sancte Spiritus!" Quickly it becomes a hymn of many voices, of yearning beauty, while everyone joins in—from Jack, the African monk over there in his white robe, to Tom and Jennifer from Germany, to Gaston from France, squatting beside the concrete pillar, to Ana from Spain, to Mirko and Jana from Croatia, to Tessa from the United States, to Enrique from El Salvador.

This beautiful call rises up to heaven as though it would never end. And almost everyone feels this hymn sink deeper and deeper into his soul, filling him with a sense of love and peace.

You can say this prayer as you prepare for Confirmation:

Come, Holy Spirit, come into my heart! Fill me utterly with your joy, your peace, your divine power. Come and live in me! Make me beautiful within. Drive from my heart all evil thoughts, all unrest, all sadness and fear. May you, O Holy Spirit, be my best friend and counselor. Guide me, so that I never stray from God's ways. May you fill me with thoughts of peace. Comfort me when I am sad. Strengthen me when I am tempted. Warm me when my love threatens to grow cold. Make me shine out with your love and be a sign for others of God's love. Veni, Sancte Spiritus!

7.7 **The fruits of the Holy Spirit**

How can you tell that the Holy Spirit is within you?
In the Letter to the Galatians Saint Paul lists nine **FRUITS OF THE HOLY SPIRIT:**

→ **Galatians 5:22–23**

LOVE (CHARITY)

Wherever the Holy Spirit is, there is Love. Love is more than mere feelings. Otherwise, we could only love an utterly sweet little baby. But we should love all babies, even the ugly or deformed ones. When the Holy Spirit kindles the love of God within us, then it's a bit like plugging into the power socket. You feel within you all the feelings that God himself has for what he has created—the people, the animals, the flowers. God is crazy with love for us. And God's love is unconditional, with no ifs and whens; it is not a passing love; it "never ends". It is utterly faithful. It transforms everything, above all the world of your relationships. With God's love inside you, you see everything with new eyes.

→ **1 Corinthians 13:8**

JOY

→ 311

What are the fruits of the Holy Spirit?

Wherever the Holy Spirit is, there is joy. Imagine a rock concert where everyone is rejoicing, dancing, waving their arms, jumping in the air. Jesus has defeated death. How cool is that, then? We are redeemed! Paradise is waiting for us. We can dance for joy, even if we still have any number of problems on our shoulders. In heaven, they tell us, the angels dance. And there is greater joy over one single person who converts and leaves all his sins behind him "than over ninety-nine righteous persons".

→ Luke 15:1–7

PEACE

99 When the peace of God has once taken root within you, then you will bring this peace to others and you will heal them of their fears and doubts.

SAINT CHARBEL MAKHLOUF

Wherever the Holy Spirit is, there is peace. All inner unrest ceases. Sadness sinks away. Fear subsides. You find your inner balance and are no longer driven about by your passions, like a leaf in the wind. Other people seek your company and your friendship because you are in harmony with yourself and with other people—and even with the animals. The peace in your heart makes you totally likeable.

PATIENCE

99 Lord, give me the strength to do everything you ask of me. Then ask of me what you will.

SAINT AUGUSTINE OF HIPPO

Wherever the Holy Spirit is, there is patience. Patience means having the courage to play the long game in life. Where others throw in the towel, you can find that extra stamina. The rapid burnout was yesterday's game. Where once you had the lungs for 800 meters, now you're a marathon runner. You can shrug off setbacks as if they're nothing. The Holy Spirit makes you into a fighter who never quits. Other people wonder where you get the strength. But you know.

SANCTE SPIRITUS!

KINDNESS

Wherever the Holy Spirit is, there is kindness. You hold the door open for someone else. You help other people with their homework. You practice in secret with someone who always bungles his volleyball serve. Mother Teresa was always reminding her sisters, who cared for the dying: "It's not enough just to care for them; you must do so with a smile!"

GOODNESS

Wherever the Holy Spirit is, there is goodness. God is all good. Doing good puts us close to God. Anyone who continually does good is automatically a "good" person—that is to say, habitually good to others. You talk to the dropout on the street corner, buy a newspaper from him. You help a child, talk to a lonely person. You spend a long time listening to an old person. You take an interest in other people's cares and worries. Living a life of goodness is the "lifestyle" of God. When people are with a good person, they can relax and blossom.

> " Nothing moves men more than love and goodness.
> SAINT CATHERINE OF SIENA

FAITHFULNESS

Wherever the Holy Spirit is, there is faithfulness. God does not change from day to day. You can count on him 100%, even when your prayers to him are sometimes answered in a rather different way than you had originally hoped. He is faithful to you, even if you betray him and other people a thousand times over. The Holy Spirit helps you to become firm-hearted and "faithful until death"—a true image of the faithful God. Have you ever read the book *The Little Prince*, by Saint-Exupéry? There is a wonderful phrase in it about faithfulness: "You become responsible forever for what you have befriended."

> " If something seems difficult to you, then remember that we are not called to be successful, but to be faithful.
> BLESSED MOTHER TERESA

GENTLENESS

Blessed
are the
meek.

Mt 5:5

Wherever the Holy Spirit is, there is gentleness. What this fruit of the Holy Spirit means is that you will have courage, but a tender courage that is not violent and does not—even in a good cause—destroy rather than build up; instead, it heals and achieves something beautiful. So you will have courage, but combined with love and patience. To bring about something great in loving patience—that is the kind of boldness that God loves. Jesus redeemed the world through a particular kind of boldness—he walked the path of nonviolence all the way to the Cross.

SELF CONTROL

Where the Holy Spirit is, there is self-control. The Holy Spirit within you enables you to be fully yourself. You will no longer be possessed by things that hold you prisoner, by people who have kept you in a state of dependency, by powerful people who order you about. You will no longer be driven by your desires, no longer be the slave of your passions. You will be free to do what your heart truly desires to do, namely, the good for which God has created you.

In addition to this list of nine fruits of the Holy Spirit, Saint Paul also mentions three others of great importance: generosity, modesty, and chastity (see Y 311).

We are threatened, not by our enemies, but by ourselves.

BLESSED CHARLES DE FOUCAULD (1858–1916, Christian hermit in the Sahara Desert)

Prayer—Staying in Touch with the Living God

From everything you've learned up to now, you know it's impossible to be a Christian without praying. That's an absolute given. Just as a love affair between a boy and a girl is not going to work if they don't ever speak words of love to each other or exchange expressions of tenderness or keep showing interest in each other. In the same way, we cannot live with God unless we daily seek to be close to him.

 The good Lord loves us to pester him.

SAINT JOHN VIANNEY
The Curé of Ars

8.1 What is prayer?

There is one person who surely knows the answer: Saint Teresa of Avila. She was a strong and passionate woman and at the same time a great mystic (which means God spoke to her in a particularly intensive manner). She is seen as perhaps the greatest teacher of prayer in the Church.

So what does Saint Teresa say that prayer is?

> Prayer, in my opinion, is nothing else than an intimate sharing between friends; it means taking time frequently to be alone with Him who we know loves us.

We can also learn from another great woman, Blessed Mother Teresa of Calcutta, how to really stay constantly in touch with God.

8.2 Learning to pray with Mother Teresa

Now you're probably going to say: Does it have to be Mother Teresa, of all people—such a great holy person? After all, I don't go straight to the world champion if I want to learn how to swim.

→ 469

What is prayer?

But don't worry. Mother Teresa had to learn to pray, just as you and I do. And there were long periods in her life when she felt as though God was far, far away from her, when she felt absolutely nothing. But one thing that Mother Teresa did understand was this: if God is very close to me, then I need to live in relationship with him. After all, he is the source of my life. Nothing happens unless God wills it. And so she sought God with an utter and tireless passion. Listen to what she has to say:

I believe there is no one who needs God more than I do. I feel so useless and weak. Because I cannot rely on myself, I rely on him, 24 hours a day. My secret is simple: I pray; I love prayer. The urge to pray is always within me. Prayer enlarges the heart until it is ready to receive God's gift of himself. We would so love to pray properly, but then we fail. If you want to pray better, pray more. If we want to be capable of loving, we must pray.

> Prayer means thinking lovingly of Jesus. Prayer is the attentiveness of the soul that concentrates on Jesus. The more one loves Jesus, the better one prays.
>
> BLESSED CHARLES DE FOUCAULD

All those who knew Mother Teresa testify that she actually did only very few things. Either she smiled and engaged with other people. Or she worked (that is, cared for one of the terminally ill or typed letters to people on a battered old Olympia typewriter). Or else she prayed. Unceasingly, the beads of her rosary slipped through her fingers. She really did strive to be in contact with God 24 hours a day. Her trust in God was immeasurable. Often she began social projects without a cent. She simply prayed and was convinced that God would not let her down. And he never did. The life of Mother Teresa is full of miracles. Suddenly, from some corner of the earth, a check would come in for exactly the amount that Mother Teresa required.

> Do what you can, and pray for what you cannot yet do. Then God will help you, so that you can do it.
>
> SAINT AUGUSTINE OF HIPPO

→ Luke 11:9–13

So now do you see why you should perhaps learn swimming from a world champion after all? Sure, we aren't likely ever to become as great at prayer as Mother Teresa. But we should at least know that genuine miracles really are possible if only we would entrust ourselves with all our hearts to God.

In the YOUCAT (p. 274) Pope Benedict invited young people to pray. He said:

> I therefore invite you every day
> to seek the Lord, who wants nothing more
> than for you to be truly happy. Foster an intense
> and constant relationship with him in prayer and,
> when possible, find suitable moments in your day to
> be alone in his company. If you do not know how to
> pray, ask him to teach you, and ask your heavenly
> Mother to pray with you and for you.

8.3 A Little School of Prayer— for all who really want to learn

In the *YOUCAT Youth Prayer Book* there is a "Little School of Prayer" that is very useful for all young people who really want to be serious about having a living relationship with God. The German playwright Berthold Brecht once said: "Truth is concrete". And even in prayer it can be seen that a person who truly seeks God is one who resolves to take concrete steps to do so. Maybe it will help you actually to write down exactly what you propose to do.

Make the decision.

God willed and created us to be free human beings. Many times a day we deliberate, set priorities, make decisions. Without decisions, nothing gets done. If you want to, make the decision to become a praying person and to shape your relationship to God. Decide deliberately ahead of time: I will pray at such and such a time. In the evening, make the decision to pray morning prayer, and in the morning to pray evening, prayer.

 → 499

When should a person pray?

Be faithful in little things.

→ 510

Is it possible to pray always?

Many begin to pray with great resolutions. After a while, they fail and think they cannot pray at all. Begin with definite, short prayer times. And keep doing it faithfully. Then your longing and your prayer, too, can grow, as it is appropriate for you, your time, and the circumstances.

Take time to pray.

Praying means being alert to the fact that God is interested in me. With him, you do not have to schedule appointments. There are three criteria for the time of your prayer that can be helpful. Choose set times (habit helps), quiet times (this is often early morning and in the evening), and valuable time that you like but are willing to give away as a gift (no "spare moments").

Prepare a place.

The place where you pray has its effect on your praying. Therefore, look for a place where you can pray well. For many people, this will be at the bedside or the desk. Others find it helpful when they have a specially prepared place that reminds and invites them: a place that has a stool or a chair with a kneeler, a carpet, an icon or picture, a candle, the Bible, a prayer book.

Rituals give structure to your prayer life.

Having to make yourself settle down to prayer every time can be a great expense of energy. Give your prayer a fixed order (a ritual). This is not supposed to restrict you but is meant, rather, to help you, so that you do not have to deliberate every day whether and how you want to pray. Before prayer, place yourself consciously in the presence of God; after prayer, take another moment to thank God for his blessings and to place yourself under his protection.

Praying is accomplished not only in thoughts and words. In prayer, the whole human person can be united with God: your body, your internal and external perception, your memory, your will, your thoughts and feelings, or the dream from last night. Even distractions often give you important information about what really concerns and motivates you and what you can intentionally bring into God's presence and leave with him. When things you need to do and don't want to forget occur to you while you're praying, you can write them down and then go back to praying.

Let the whole person pray.

Discover and practice the many ways of praying, which can vary depending on the time, one's frame of mind, and the present situation: a prayer composed by someone else with which I join in; personal prayer about my own concerns; praying with a passage from Sacred Scripture (for example the readings from Mass for the day); the prayer of the heart (or "Jesus Prayer"), in which a short prayer formula or simply the name "Jesus" is repeated with each breath; interior prayer, in which the whole person is silent and listens internally and externally.

Pray in a variety of ways.

 → 491

Can you learn to pray from the Bible?

You can also make use of the opportunities that arise to pray at in-between times (for example, short, fervent prayers, a petition, a prayer of thanksgiving or praise): while waiting, while riding on the bus, the train or in the car (instead of turning the music on right away), during free time, while visiting a chapel or church along your daily walk. Let the opportunities you have to pray become invitations to unite yourself again and again with God.

Use the opportunities.

 → 498

Can you pray anywhere?

Let God speak.

Praying also means listening to God's voice. God speaks most explicitly in the words of Sacred Scripture, which the Church reads day after day. He speaks through the Tradition of the Church and the witness of the saints. But he also speaks—often in a hidden way—in the heart of every man, for instance in the judgment of your conscience or through an interior joy. God's Word in Scripture makes it possible to hear the Word of God in the heart and lends a voice to it. Give God a chance to speak in your prayer. Become familiar with him, so that you can learn to tell his voice apart from the many other voices and come to know his will.

Pray with the Church on earth and in heaven

→ 492

Does my personal prayer have something to do with the prayer of the Church?

Anyone who prays—whether alone or with others—enters into the great community of those who pray. It extends from earth to heaven and includes those who are alive today and also the angels, the saints, and the unknown multitude of those who live with God. Praying also means praying for each other. Therefore, it is good to pray not only by yourself but also, when possible, with others: with your family, with friends, with your congregation—and with the saints. You can ask them for their prayers. For in God's sight the community of those who pray does not cease with death.

8.4 **The two most important prayers in the world**

The two most important prayers in the world are the **OUR FATHER** and the **HAIL MARY**. The Our Father because Jesus himself gave us these words to say, and the Hail Mary because it begins with the words used by the angel of God to proclaim the Incarnation of Christ. Not a single day should pass without your walking in the footsteps of these prayers—your whole life long.

But don't simply rattle them off thoughtlessly; rather, meditate again and again on what they mean. On the following pages is an attempt to put these two prayers into a new language—only for meditation, not for actually praying them out loud. Theologians will no doubt have many comments to make on our translation. However, it is important for you to try, with the help of your parish priest or catechist, to penetrate more deeply into the meaning of the words, which will accompany for all your life. And you must approach these prayers with your heart.

 → **491**

What does it mean to learn from Jesus how to pray?

The Our Father

→ 511–527

What are the words of the Our Father?

Our Father who art in heaven,
>Invisible Father of all mankind,

hallowed be thy name.
>We want to praise your greatness;

Thy kingdom come.
>May your new life show itself everywhere!

Thy will be done on earth as it is in heaven.
>May your wishes be fulfilled everywhere,
>in the visible and the invisible realms!

Give us this day our daily bread,
>Give us, day by day, what we need to live on;

and forgive us our trespasses,
>do not treat us according to what we have done wrong;
>grant us a new beginning,

as we forgive those who trespass against us,
>just as we also give a second chance
>to those who have done something to hurt us;

and lead us not into temptation,
>and do not leave us to face temptation alone,

but deliver us from evil.
>But free us from evil.

**[For the kingdom, the power, and the glory are yours,
now and for ever.**
>For with you everything is as it should be; you can do everything! With you, joy never ends.]

Amen.
>Yes, that is true.

You can pray...

...standing   ...sitting   ...kneeling   ...or prostrate on the ground

More here:

 → 486

The Hail Mary

Hail, Mary,
full of grace,
The Lord is with thee.
Blessed art thou among women,
and blessed is the fruit
of thy womb,

Jesus.

Holy Mary,
Mother of God,
pray for us sinners

now
and at the hour of our death.

Amen.

Hello, Mary,
you are full of divine power.
God is with you.
You are more greatly blessed
than all women in the world;
and the greatest blessing is what fills
your womb:

Jesus.

Holy Mary,
Mother of the God-made-man,
pray for us who have failed before God,
at this moment
and also when we die.

Yes, let it be so.

 → 480

What are the words of the "Hail Mary"?

AN OLD WOMAN WITH PLENTY OF WRINKLES

9 The Church—a Home for You and Me

Many people go on forever finding fault with the Church. They come up with a whole collection of things—about all the stuff the Church has done in the 2,000 years of her existence and about all the scandals that are in the Church still. Many of these critics are people who have been baptized and therefore belong to the Church themselves. The famous theologian Karl Rahner (1904–1984) once took them to task about this, saying: *"The Church is an old woman with many wrinkles and blemishes. But she is* my *mother. And you don't hit a mother."* And he is right. The Church is our mother. She has given us the gift of new life; she nourishes us with the Word of God and with the sacraments. Without the Church, we would none of us have our faith. We would be still groping around in the darkness, forced to try and redeem ourselves—which is impossible.

→ **121**
What does "Church" mean?

→ **347**
Why is "not practicing what you preach" such a serious deficiency in a Christian?

9.1 The Church is not a club for the perfect

Yes, it is true. The scandals in the Church are and remain shameful and a real outrage. And yet they are not simply random flaws that can be eliminated with a bit of effort and goodwill. Bernhard Meuser wrote this in his book *Christianity for Beginners:*

→ **343**
How does the Church help us to lead a good, responsible life?

"Jesus himself associated with ordinary and even quite dangerous people; he was willing to engage one-on-one with the ill-reputed Mary Magdalen, with the tax collector and cheat Zacchaeus, with a woman caught in the act of adultery, with bad people like Judas, who later betrayed him, with Peter, who denied him three times before the cock crowed twice. If only the purest of the pure were allowed to belong to the Church, then it would probably be empty. At any rate, I myself would have no chance of finding a place within her. I know myself, and I wouldn't put anything past me. The flesh-and-blood Church ... is not a club for the perfect, but rather what Jesus wanted her to be—a place for the slow transformation of quite ordinary people. People who maybe misbehave from time to time, who have a lot to answer for, who urgently need to be taken by the scruff of the neck and straightened out.

→ **Mark 2:17**

Fortunately for us, Jesus has assured us that it is "not the healthy who need the doctor, but the sick" and that "I have come to call sinners, not the righteous ..." We all have our particular weak points in life—for one person it might be money, for another truthfulness, for another sex; a fourth person may be unreliable, a fifth being pigheaded, and the sixth: there I am. We don't simply stride ahead in a triumphal march. Instead, we hobble, limp, creep forward. But we are moving. And we're doing so together. That's the kind of Church in which I feel at home."

" Mary is the Mother and model of the Church.

POPE BENEDICT XVI

9.2 If you want to understand the mystery of the Church

If you want to understand the innermost mystery of the Church, then look at this picture for a moment:

At first glance, it is a picture of Mary. But since earliest times Mary has been regarded as the "Mother of the Church". Why? Because her body was the first dwelling place of the incarnate Son of God. More than this: Jesus was the entire meaning of Mary's life. She was around him; he was in her. That is exactly how the Church must be—a place in which the RISEN LORD can work today. A place of perfect love and willing service: "Let it be done to me according to thy word", was Mary's response when the angle revealed God's will to her. God was seeking a place where he could dwell in this world. In fact, it was not only then that God was seeking a place where Jesus could live his earthly life. For he continues to seek this place today, in you and me.

The Church has no other meaning to her existence but Jesus himself. We must only be there—around Jesus—and allow him to work within us. Then we are the Church. At one point in Saint Luke's Gospel, Jesus says: "My mother and my brethren are those who hear the word of God and do it" (Lk 8:21). "The Church", said Pope Benedict XVI, "is God's family in the world."

And so the Church is first of all the living Jesus himself, who lives among us today—and only then does she include his

> " You yourselves are the Body of Christ, the Church! Bring the undiminished fire of your love into this Church whose countenance has so often been disfigured by man.
>
> BENEDICT XVI
> Foreword to the
> YOUCAT

"family", only then does she include us, imperfect, handicapped, sinners, who are permitted to be "one body" together with Jesus. And now perhaps you can better understand what it means when we are told:

9.3 You are the body of Christ

Jesus has associated himself so profoundly with us that we are now, in some sense, "one body" with him. This is underlined by the Bible in many places. Saint Augustine of Hippo (350–430) said something very profound about what happens when we receive Holy Communion: "To that which you are you respond 'Amen' ('yes, it is true!'), and, by responding to it, you assent to it. For you hear the words 'the Body of Christ' and respond 'Amen'. Be then a member of the Body of Christ, that your Amen may be true."

→ 126

What does it mean to say that the Church is the "Body of Christ"?

Look around at the other people in your group. They are your brothers and sisters. Wow! That means that in some way you are "one body", that they are like a part of you! Our faith in Jesus binds us together more closely than the natural bond with our father and mother or our natural brothers and sisters.

→ 1 Corinthians 12:12–28

The most important passage in the Bible about the Church as the "Body of Christ" comes from the First Letter of Saint Paul to the Corinthians. Read it closely and try to discover ...

💧 What you receive from other members of the Body of Christ
💧 and what role you might play within the Body of Christ.
💧 What are your particular gifts?
💧 For what do your sisters and brothers need you?

9.4 You are the temple of the Holy Spirit

Another important image of the Church is "Temple of the Holy Spirit". The word "temple" means something like a "sacred space". God is present everywhere, of course, but it is often difficult to distinguish when we are dealing with something divine and when with something merely human.

→ 128

What does it mean to say that the Church is the "Temple of the Holy Spirit"?

It is fascinating to read in Sacred Scripture that God truly wishes to "live" among us. Your task and mine is to make a "livable" place for God within us.

→ 2 Corinthians 6:16
→ Ephesians 2:20–22

But it is not only we ourselves who are supposed to build a temple. That is something that many people have worked on

together. And ultimately it is the Holy Spirit who works day and night building up the dwelling place of God among us.

9.5 You are the People of God

At the Second Vatican Council (1962–1965), an ancient biblical image of the Church was revived, namely, the image of the "People of God", which, "like a stranger in a foreign land, presses forward amid the persecutions of the world and the consolations of God". Originally, the People of God meant the people of Israel, with their long history with God. Now, in Jesus Christ, people from all nations and cultures are called to follow the path to God.

This wonderful message is explained in the First Letter of Saint Peter.

→ 125

What is unique about the People of God?

→ 1 Peter 2:7–10

9.6 A little bit of organization

When we look at the Church today, we are almost dumbfounded by what has become of her in 2,000 years. We could so easily lose sight of what she really is.

- 🖑 Sometimes we look at the *vast institution*; we see her great churches and cathedrals, her administrative apparatus, official structures, and social institutions.
- 🖑 Then again we look at the *spiritual reality* of the Church: we hear of vocations and see people who pray or even give their whole lives to God.

The two realities belong together—the **SPIRITUAL** and the **INSTITUTIONAL.** Without the institution, the Church could not exist in the world. She needs money to be able to help others, buildings to provide spaces where people can meet, and people to carry out a specific role or function. But the whole thing would be merely a dead, empty structure if the **SPIRITUAL DIMENSION**—God's living reality in the Holy Spirit—were not part of how the Church. If you want to know how the Church is structured, read about it in YOUCAT.

→ 138

How is the one, holy, catholic, and apostolic Church structured?

And what is the point of it all?

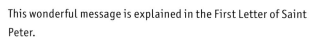

The Church does not exist for her own sake. God would not take the least pleasure in her if she merely revolved around herself. He has created the Church for the sake of mankind. She is meant to be a "sign and instrument both of a very closely knit union with God and of the unity of the whole human race." (Second Vatican Council).

The Church is serving her purpose if she fulfills three fundamental duties:

She must proclaim the Word of God.

→ 2 Timothy 4:2

She must administer the sacraments and celebrate the Holy Eucharist.

→ 123

What is the task
of the Church?

She must serve all mankind in love.

→ Matthew 25:40

WHAT A GIFT!

Eucharist—the
Generosity of God

10

Many young people don't like going to Holy Mass. Some of them say, "It's the wrong type of music, and they're the wrong type of people!" Others simply say, "I find it all completely boring." And they prefer just to stay in bed—especially since many parents themselves don't go to Holy Mass. Read about "kiss duty" in YOUCAT sometime (page 131)!

→ 219
How often must a Catholic Christian participate in the celebration of the Eucharist?

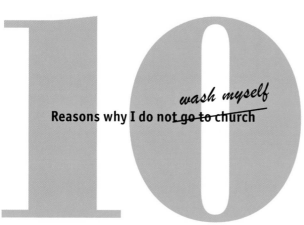

Reasons why I do not ~~go to church~~ *wash myself*

1. As a child I was made to wash.
2. People who keep on washing are hypocrites who think they are cleaner than other people.
3. There are so many different sorts of soap. How am I supposed to know which is the best one for me?
4. All the water companies are simply after our money.
5. I've tried washing from time to time, but it was always so boring and always the same.
6. It's always so cold and uninviting in the bathroom.
7. I do wash at Christmas and Easter. Surely that's enough!
8. None of my friends seems to think it's necessary to wash.
9. I really don't have time to wash.
10. Maybe I'll wash one day, when I'm older.

→ 345
What are the "Five Precepts of the Church"?

So we need to have some very good arguments if we are going to put this appointment right at the top of our list of priorities.

In the Eucharist, God gives us the greatest gift in the world. He gives himself—to you and to me.

> All that I have and possess, you have given to me.
>
> SAINT IGNATIUS OF LOYOLA

We human beings often have great difficulty with giving and receiving. Sometimes our giving can be almost a form of blackmail. And sometimes a gift is simply a "thing" that someone wants to get rid of. He simply ties a bow around it and gives it to me. And now I'm stuck with the trash. That's why some people really don't like accepting gifts. They say, "I'd rather buy myself something. Then I know what I have and don't feel under any obligation to anyone!" Or, "I don't want to have to say 'thank you' to anyone."

Ask yourself if you'd really like to live in a world in which everything is only a matter of money or of simply having a right to certain things. Would you like it if no one ever gave you anything anymore? Would it make you happy if you never had to think of doing something nice for anyone anymore? Then you could simply erase the word "thank you" from your vocabulary.

Surely, such a world would be a nightmare—a cold and inhuman world. It would also be an atheistic (that is, a godless) world.

→ 1 Corinthians 4:7

For God can only give. He has created the world in freedom and out of love. He has given you and me the gift of life. Each day he gives us the closeness of his presence. If God were to stop giving to us, we would be lost. We live from his giving, from his blessing. Men have always known this.

10.1 **Little gifts to nurture friendship?**
We need blessings ... when the weather is bad and the harvest is poor and hunger stalks the city. And not only that: at times we may be threatened by enemies, or plagues and epidemics may rage. That is why, in almost every race and every culture, people have offered sacrifice to a god or

gods. They would say to themselves: Surely, it can't hurt to get ourselves on the right side of such "higher powers"? And so people would often take the very best and most precious of what they had: say, part of the harvest or, quite often, the "first fruits"—young unblemished animals—and offer these in sacrifice to their gods. In fact, the Aztecs (and they were not the only ones) even offered human sacrifices to their sun god. They saw how the huge, blood-red fireball would sink behind the mountains, and they feared that this sun god might not rise again unless it were fed with blood.

And so, offering sacrifice ...

 might, on the one hand, be a beautiful gesture of gratitude to a god who sustains life and sends blessings; however ...

 on the other hand, it might be a desperate attempt to bribe and placate some grotesque monster that is perceived as a "god".

10.2 God—a master of giving

God is not someone who gives and then jealously waits and watches, expecting to be given something in return. The only thing that God wants from us is our loving hearts and our gratitude.

God is the most unselfish giver in all the world. And the most generous. As Saint Augustine says (YOUCAT p. 187), "God never gives less than himself." And the greatest gift God has given us is Jesus. The way in which Jesus has made himself into a gift for you and me is what we call "Eucharist".

"Eucharist" (Greek = thanksgiving), as the YOUCAT tells us, "was at first the name for the prayer of thanksgiving that preceded the transformation of the bread and wine into Christ's Body and Blood in the liturgy of the early Church. Later the term was applied to the whole celebration of the Mass" (YOUCAT, p. 122).

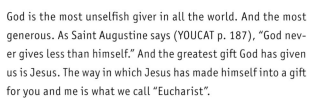

> God desires you more than he desires your gifts.
>
> SAINT AUGUSTINE OF HIPPO

→ Psalm 51:19

→ 208
What is Holy Eucharist?

→ p. 122

99 Let us thank God for everything, since all good comes from him.

SAINT FRANCIS OF ASSISI

When we celebrate "Eucharist", this is creation's great thanksgiving to God. Each time Holy Mass is celebrated, we hear the words, *"It is truly right and just, our duty and our salvation, always and everywhere to give you thanks, Lord, holy Father, almighty and eternal God, through Christ our Lord ..."*

From the earth a great song of joy rises up to God. Jesus is the center of this jubilation—Jesus, who gives us the gift of his life and restores the redeemed creation back to God.

 ### How Jesus gave himself to us

The story actually begins when Jesus sets out to celebrate the feast of Passover and the Paschal meal, together with his disciples, in Jerusalem. This was nothing unusual, in fact. All Jewish families who could afford to do so would travel up to Jerusalem for the Passover feast in order to commemorate in a special festival the famous night of the EXODUS, in which Israel was freed from Egyptian slavery.

Flashback:

→ Exodus 12

That night the Israelites had been commanded to slaughter an unblemished one-year-old lamb and to smear its blood on the doorposts and lintel of their houses. When the angel of death saw the blood, he would "pass over" the house.

By the time of Jesus, precise instructions had been passed down about the way in which this solemn Passover meal was to be held. The father of the household, or the head of the

clan, played an important role in it. Let us imagine Jesus in this role:

→ 99
What happened at the Last Supper?

- 🔥 The leader had to proclaim a "eucharist"—a prayer of thanksgiving to the "King of the world, who has brought forth bread from the earth".
- 🔥 Then he had to bless a special chalice filled with wine, while thanking the Lord "who has created the fruit of the vine".
- 🔥 He had to offer an unblemished, one-year-old lamb in sacrifice.
- 🔥 This lamb had to be slaughtered at a precise time ...
- 🔥 and it had to be in the Temple in Jerusalem.
- 🔥 The hour of the sacrificial slaughter was on Good Friday at 3:00 P.M.

Now read the description given by the evangelist Luke of the meal that Jesus celebrated with the apostles in Jerusalem.

Saint John the Evangelist emphasized the fact that the meal took place one day before the feast of Passover. If you compare the instructions above with the report of Saint Luke and the words of Saint John, can you spot the five "mistakes" made by Jesus? What did he do differently?

→ Luke 22:14–20

10.4 The five "mistakes" of Jesus

Of course Jesus didn't make any "mistakes", but if we identify the five changes he made, then we begin to have some

idea of what the gift actually was that Jesus was preparing for us at the Last Supper and in his death:

→ 209

When did Christ institute the Eucharist?

🌢 The **first** change was in the time. It seems that Jesus celebrated the Pasch exactly one day earlier than everyone else. That's like celebrating New Year's Day on New Year's Eve. So why did Jesus celebrate it on the day we now know as "Holy Thursday"? Well, on Good Friday, he poured out his blood for us, outside the city, on the Cross—at about 3 P.M., in fact. This was the very time when the Temple of Jerusalem was swimming in blood because of the thousands upon thousands of lambs being sacrificed there. In this way, Jesus was telling us: I am the one Sacrifice that reconciles heaven and earth.

🌢 The **second** change is not expressly stated in the text, but it can be seen in numerous paintings of the Last Supper. Jesus did indeed celebrate with bread and wine, but there is no Paschal lamb to be seen in these paintings. To commemorate the Passover without a lamb?—that's impossible … By excluding the lamb, these paintings point to Jesus himself as the Lamb. By excluding mention of a lamb, the Gospel texts describing the Last Supper shift our focus to

→ John 1:29

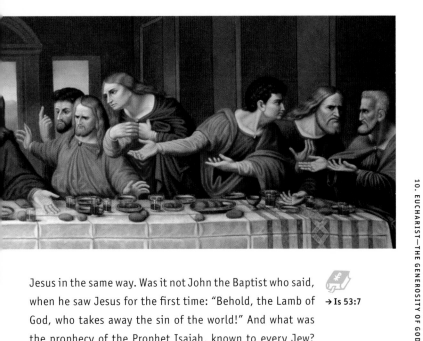

Jesus in the same way. Was it not John the Baptist who said, when he saw Jesus for the first time: "Behold, the Lamb of God, who takes away the sin of the world!" And what was the prophecy of the Prophet Isaiah, known to every Jew? "He was oppressed, and he was afflicted, yet he opened not his mouth; like a lamb that is led to the slaughter, and like a sheep that before its shearers is silent, so he opened not his mouth."

→ Is 53:7

The **third** change consists in what Jesus actually did with the bread and wine. Of the bread he said: "This is my body." And of the wine he said: "This is my blood." Ever since then, this transformation has taken place in every Holy Mass. It is about complete and utter transformation, transformation of the entire creation and also my transformation from a sinful, mortal being into a being who will no longer die. But why does it begin with bread? Because Jesus wished to be the new manna in the desert (the "food which endures to eternal life") by means of which man can survive death. And why with wine? "I am the vine, you are the branches", Jesus had said before. "He who abides in me, and I in him, he it is that bears much fruit, for apart from me you can do nothing" (Jn 15:5). His blood is, so to speak, to course

→ 210

How did Jesus institute the Eucharist?

Our sharing in the body and blood of Christ has no other end than that we should be transformed into what we receive.

POPE LEO THE GREAT

through our veins like enlivening wine. "We are to become the Body of Christ", said Pope Benedict XVI, "his own Flesh and Blood."

→ John 15:13

🔥 The **fourth** change was this: Jesus associated the breaking of the bread with himself. Just as this bread had to be broken so that it could be distributed to everyone, so it was to be with him, also. His body would be broken; it would be "given for you". He would offer up the last drop of his blood, "poured out for you". In Saint John's Gospel, Jesus says, "Greater love has no man than this, that a man lay down his life for his friends."

🔥 The **fifth** change was this: Jesus transformed the Paschal meal when he said: "Do this in memory of me." For the Jews, the Paschal meal was a sacred remembrance of God, their liberator from slavery in Egypt. Now Jesus was either placing himself in God's place (and thereby committing, in Jewish eyes, a crime punishable by death) or he was indeed the Son of God who was preparing for a still greater act of liberation than the Exodus from Egypt ever was: He would die so that we might have life.

So it was that the Paschal meal of Jesus became the core of the Holy Mass, in which Jesus gives himself forever anew to us.

🔩 10.5 What do we get out of it?

Sometimes, when they're given a present, people ask themselves: "What good is that to me?" When it comes to the Eucharist, YOUCAT has a good answer.

→ 217

What happens in the Church when she celebrates the Eucharist?

Not long ago a priest was asked by some young people if he had a very simple explanation of the Eucharist. "Yes, I do", said the priest. "It's like in a marriage. The most meaningful thing that the two can do is give each other their bodies and their sufferings. And quite possibly it's the sufferings that they have endured—with each other and for each other—that bind them most closely together. In the Eucharist, it is exactly the same. Jesus says to me: I give you my body—that is to say, my life—and I give you my sufferings. And I say to Jesus: Then I want to give you my life and my sufferings, too!" The young people looked very thoughtful. And the priest went on: "That's how I see it every day when I celebrate Holy Mass."

A smuggler's story

In the year 2011 Father Johannes Prassek, a priest from the town of Lubeck in northern Germany, was beatified.

He was executed by the Nazis for "treasonably assisting the enemy". During the long months of his imprisonment, the thing he missed most of all was the Blessed Eucharist. Finally, one brave person managed to smuggle in a couple of hosts and a little wine to the young priest in his prison, along with a food parcel. "If you only knew how much joy it brought me!" Father Prassek wrote back secretly. "The food, of course; but most of all the hosts and the wine. I sobbed like a little child, for sheer joy. Now I celebrate Holy Mass here every morning—so simply that it could scarcely have been simpler even in the catacombs. A salt bowl is the chalice, a handkerchief is the corporal [the cloth on which the chalice is placed]. Only a few drops of wine and a tiny piece of the host, so that both will last for many times. Thank you for having had the courage to think of such a thing."

> "Jesus does not demand great deeds. All He wants is self-surrender and gratitude.... He needs nothing from us except our love."
>
> SAINT THÉRÈSE OF LISIEUX

> "Whoever receives the sacred Eucharist loses himself in God like a drop of water in the ocean. No one can separate them from each other again. If someone were to surprise us, after our Holy Communion, with the question: "What are you taking back home with you?" then we could answer: "We are taking heaven back with us."
>
> SAINT JOHN VIANNEY
> Curé of Ars

Johannes Prassek was going to his death. But he had a remedy against death and fear—the "Bread of life" that is Jesus.

WE NEED TO TALK TOGETHER, PART II.

11 Update! Confession!

You can imagine what would happen if you didn't update your computer for months on end. Sooner or later, the operating system would grind to a halt. Or else there would be some serious gaps in your security. The firewall would no longer work, and viruses and Trojans could start to wreak havoc on your PC— and in the end, all your data would be corrupted.

 → 224

Why did Christ give us the sacrament of Penance and the Anointing of the Sick?

"I don't need any forgiveness, and I certainly don't need confession!"—Such a remark is about as dumb as saying, "I don't need any updates. My software is running okay as it is."

You could say that God has created us a bit like a wonderful piece of software. But this software still needs regular updates. And if you don't make use of these updates, then even the best system will crash in time. **CONFESSION**—which is also called the "sacrament of Reconciliation"—is the comprehensive "update system" provided by God.

 → 225

What names are there for the sacrament of Penance?

11.1 The thing that messes you up

The thing that messes you up is sin. Sin is not only the bad things we do but also the good things we don't do. So sin is not only the anger, the unkindness, the envy, the many little faults we commit. Sin is also the fact that we could have helped and didn't; the fact that we have certain talents but were too lazy to use them; the fact that we could have helped a good cause to victory but, instead, we simply ran away like cowards.

 → 226

But we have Baptism, which reconciles us with God; why then do we need a special sacrament of Reconciliation?

All these different sins and omissions act like viruses in a PC. They make our lives slow, sad, and ugly. One sin tends to bring another in its wake. Bad habits creep in. Often we imagine that, with a little bit of goodwill, we can fix it by ourselves. But the truth is, we're kidding ourselves! After the umpteenth attempt to overcome our uncharitable ways, we tend to give in, resign ourselves, and often try to cover up, or "overwrite", our sinfulness. And besides, we tell ourselves, our sins aren't really that bad ...

11.2 How God gives us a new beginning

Every sin we commit is ultimately a sin against God himself. He has created us so marvelously. And yet what do we do with this gift? We stand by and let it slowly become dirtied and disfigured. That is not what God wants. He gives us a unique chance to make our life once again as beautiful and powerful as it was at the moment when we were created by God, as his beloved children.

→ 228

Who can forgive sins?

The story of the "Prodigal Son" is one of the most wonderful stories in the whole Bible—though we would do better to call it the story of the "merciful Father". It shows us a God who is so full of love and kindness that even in the worst messes we can make of things, we still cannot stop him from loving us.

→ Luke 15:11–32

Maybe your sins aren't quite as bad as those of the Prodigal Son. But even then, you still need God to embrace you in his great love and help you to start over again. For "though your sins are like scarlet, they shall be as white as snow." So follow your longing to be made altogether perfect and beautiful by God once more. Overcome your reluctance, and go to Confession—above all now that you want to be confirmed! And remember: even priests have to go to Confession; even the pope himself regularly kneels in the confessional in order to confess his sins and failings to some simple, ordinary priest and to be reconciled with God once more. Imagine the man who has to listen to the sins of the pope!

→ Isaiah 1:18

11.3 What makes a good Confession?

Maybe you have a somewhat distorted idea of the way Confession goes: You creep into the confessional box—or confession room; you reel off your sins, listen while some words are recited; then you leave. Only thing worse is the dentist. But let's take another, calmer look at it. The YOUCAT tells us what is absolutely necessary for a proper confession.

→ 232

What must I bring to a confession?

11.4 What sorts of things should I confess, then?

In order to find out where my life has gone a bit off the tracks and no longer reflects the love of God, it helps to make a so-called "examination of conscience". This involves thinking about one's actions in light of a list of God's commandments. But you can find many other kinds, for example, on the Internet. Here is a very good one, written especially for young people:

 → 349

What are the Ten Commandments?

Sin is not only when I act without love, but also when I look inwardly, at myself alone, and do not allow myself first of all to be loved by God. For if I reject his infinite love, then I myself become loveless.

If I enjoy the good things of life, that's no sin; but it is a sin if I make them into my god and try to get hold of them at all costs.

 → 315

What is a sin in the first place?

If I want to earn a decent wage, that's no sin. But it is a sin if I make wealth my one and only aim. And if I'm unwilling to share and have a heart for others for fear of missing out on life.

 → 294

Is someone a sinner if he experiences strong passions within himself?

If I insist on my rights, that's no sin. But it is a sin if I abuse these rights, if I become inconsiderate and hardhearted or disrespect the rights of others.

If I experience sexual desires and impulses, that's no sin. But it is a sin if I give way to my impulses or use others to satisfy my desires.

 → 291

How can a person tell whether his action is good or bad?

If I find it hard to like some people, that's no sin. But it is a sin if I treat them as though they were not God's beloved children every bit as much as I am.

 → 396

How does a Christian deal with anger?

If I criticize other people, that's not necessarily a sin. But it is a sin if I do so hastily or without charity or if I thereby demean or injure other people.

 → 466

What is envy, and how can you fight against it?

If feelings of envy, malice, or anger rise up within me, that's not in itself a sin. But it is a sin if I do not try to overcome these feelings but, instead, let my actions be influenced by them.

If I talk about others, that's no sin. But it is a sin if I gossip about others or say mean or spiteful things about them.

 → 455

What does it mean to be truthful?

If I keep silent in situations of conflict, that's no sin. But it is a sin if I keep silent when others are being disparaged, slandered, or lied about.

If I get into arguments, that's not necessarily a sin. But it is a sin if I pick a quarrel, don't listen to others, don't try to understand them, or am unwilling to make peace.

If my heart often seems empty when I pray, that's no sin. But it is a sin if I think I don't need to pray or if I don't even take the trouble to open my heart to God and listen for his voice.

 → 508

What happens if you do not feel anything when you pray or even experience reluctance to pray?

If I am sometimes unsure of my faith, that's no sin. But it is a sin if I withdraw from the community of believers, if I regularly refuse to take part in their worship, or if I think earthly things more important than heavenly ones.

If I make plans for my life, that's no sin. But it is a sin if my faith in God plays no part in them, if I no longer care about the fact that my life each day lies in his hands.

12 What Happens in Confirmation?

If you have followed this Confirmation course up to now and worked through this book, then you will know that the most important part of your Confirmation is not the expensive watch or the laptop that some kind person may perhaps give you, but the moment of the Confirmation itself, in which something happens between heaven and earth, between your God and you.

> God, who created you without you, will not save you without you.
>
> SAINT AUGUSTINE OF HIPPO

- You will say **YES** to the gift of God, the Holy Spirit
- He will come into your life ...
- and he will never again leave you, not even in the moment of your departure from this earth, for he loves you without end.

After the bishop has given his homily, you will profess your faith before him. Without faith, no one can receive any of the sacraments. And if you really wish to receive the Holy Spirit, then you must renounce everything that is opposed to God. That is why the bishop (or his representative) will ask all the Confirmation candidates:

→ 203
What is Confirmation?

The bishop:	**Do you renounce Satan and all his works and all his empty show?**
The candidates: (together): **I do.**	

After the negative, now comes the positive:

The bishop:	**Do you believe in God, the Father almighty, Creator of heaven and earth?**
The candidates:	**I do.**

The bishop:	**Do you believe in Jesus Christ, his only Son, our Lord, who was born of the Virgin Mary, suffered death and was buried, rose again from the dead and is seated at the right hand of the Father?**
The candidates:	**I do.**

Then the bishop will ask you if you are really serious about the Church:

The bishop: **Do you believe in the Holy Spirit, the Lord, the giver of life, who came upon the Apostles at Pentecost and today is given to you sacramentally in Confirmation?**

The candidates: **I do.**

The bishop: **Do you believe in the holy Catholic Church, the communion of saints, the forgiveness of sins, the resurrection of the body, and life everlasting?**

The candidates: **I do.**

Then the bishop confirms your profession of faith:

The bishop: **This is our faith. This is the faith of the Church. We are proud to profess it in Christ Jesus our Lord.**

 → 118

 → Acts 2

Now follows the invitation to all those present to pray together. It is a little like that first Pentecost, when the infant Church had gathered together around Mary and fervently prayed for the coming of the Holy Spirit. And as you know, moments later tongues of fire descended upon them! So in the following words the bishop invites the whole congregation to pray together:

The bishop: **My dear friends, in Baptism God our Father gave the new birth of eternal life to his chosen sons and daughters. Let us pray to our Father that he will pour out the Holy Spirit to strengthen his sons and daughters with his gifts and anoint them to be more like Christ the Son of God.**

All pray in silence for a short time, fervently and from their hearts. It's best if the people kneel at this moment, since kneeling is a posture of especially intense prayer.

Then the bishop extends his hands over the candidates. By this gesture, the bishop draws together and gives voice to the profound prayers of all present. He uses the following words:

The bishop: **All-powerful God, Father of our Lord Jesus Christ, by water and the Holy Spirit you freed your sons and daughters from sin and gave them new life. Send your Holy Spirit upon them to be their helper and guide. Give them the spirit of wisdom and understanding, the spirit of right judgment and courage, the spirit of knowledge and reverence. Fill them with the spirit of wonder and awe in your presence. We ask this through Christ our Lord.**

→ 310
What are the seven gifts of the Holy Spirit?

All respond: **Amen.** (Which means: So be it; we ask this too!)

Now follows the actual anointing. A deacon or another helper brings the chrism to the bishop.

Chrism

is a sacred, perfumed ointment, consisting of olive oil mixed with the wonderful fragrance of balsam. In the past, in Israel, they would anoint kings, priests, and prophets with chrism. Jesus himself is known as "the Christ". This is a Greek term and basically means "the anointed one". Incidentally, the Hebrew word for "the anointed one" is the "Messiah". Since they now belong to Christ, the confirmation candidates share in the dignity of Christ, the great Priest, King, and Prophet. The beautiful perfume of the chrism also has a symbolic significance: it means that the candidates have the duty to spread (or bear witness to) the "fragrance of the knowledge of Christ", namely, the gospel.

"" God has created me to do Him some definite service; He has committed some work to me which He has not committed to another. I have my mission—I may never know it in this life, but I shall be told it in the next.... I am a link in a chain, a bond of connexion between persons.

BLESSED JOHN HENRY NEWMAN

The role of your sponsor

is very ancient. It was introduced in the very earliest days of the Church. It is very important for you, together with your parents, to choose a really good Confirmation sponsor. The person chosen has always been a Catholic Christian, of good standing, who has lived his faith in an exemplary manner. So it shouldn't really be old, deep-pocketed Uncle Joe, who doesn't have a clue about the faith but might well treat you to a gold watch ... It doesn't even have to be a relative of yours. It might possibly be a young adult who is involved in the Catholic Church and could be a model for you to follow. You see, your sponsor is not simply someone to accompany you on the day of your Confirmation. The cool outing and the nice big present are about as important for your Confirmation as the baubles

The candidates, accompanied by their sponsors, now approach the bishop individually.

The sponsor places his or her right hand on your shoulder and gives your name to the bishop. Sometimes it is the candidate himself who is asked to give this name.

The bishop dips his right thumb in the chrism, places his hand on your head and makes the Sign of the Cross with his thumb on your forehead.

The bishop addresses you by your name and says:

N., be sealed with the Gift of the Holy Spirit.

on the Christmas tree are for Christmas—in other words, not at all. Though of course they're nice, nonetheless. The job of your sponsor is above all to accompany you as you grow in your life and in your faith—in other words, a little bit like your own personal "coach", given by a loving God.

In order to symbolize his acceptance of this duty before the whole community, your sponsor stands behind you at the moment of your Confirmation and places his right hand on your shoulder. In order to fulfill the formal requirements of the Church, sponsors must (a) be at least 16 years old, (b) have been baptized and confirmed, (c) be a member of the Catholic Church, (d) live a life in accordance with the Catholic faith and appropriate to the duty they have taken on.

You reply:

Amen.

This means something like:

Yes, so be it. I want this.
I agree to this.

The bishop then says:

Peace be with you.

The newly confirmed responds:

And with your spirit.

So now you are confirmed.

After this, a number of prayers (intercessions) are offered for the newly confirmed for their parents and sponsors, for the whole Church, and for all mankind. But the crucial point is the seal of the Holy Spirit on your forehead. At the World Youth Day in Sydney, Pope Benedict explained to the young people there what it means to receive this sign on your forehead:

What does it mean to
receive the "seal" of the Holy Spirit?
It means being indelibly marked, inalterably
changed, a new creation. For those who have received this gift, nothing can ever be the same! Being
"baptized" in the one Spirit means being set on fire
with the love of God. Being "given to drink" of the Spirit
means being refreshed by the beauty of the Lord's plan
for us and for the world and becoming in turn a source of
spiritual refreshment for others. Being "sealed with the
Spirit" means not being afraid to stand up for Christ,
letting the truth of the gospel permeate the
way we see, think, and act, as we work for the
triumph of the civilization of love.

→ cf.
**1 Corinthians
12:13**

Make the most of it! God is with you.

Sources

The examination of conscience is taken from the German pamphlet entitled *Sünde ist ... die Liebe leugnen* (Sin means ... denying love), edited by Bernhard Riedl (Archdiocese of Cologne, 2008).

YOUCAT School of Prayer is taken from:
YOUCAT Youth Prayer Book, edited by Georg von Lengerke and Dörte Schrömges (San Francisco: Ignatius Press, 2013).

10 Reasons Why I Don't Wash (10 Gründe warum ich mich nicht wasche) from the *YOUCAT Youth Calendar 2013*, edited by Norbert Fink (Augsburg, 2012).

Quotation in the section "The Church is not a club for the perfect" taken from *Christ sein für Einsteiger*, by Bernhard Meuser (Munich, 2007).

Photographs

Jessica Abu Haydar 86; Lisa Barber 8; Tobias Bunk 106; Maria Clara Costa 35; picture-
alliance / dpa 38; Andreas Düren 68; Dirk Egger, JUGEND2000 Regensburg 101;
fisherman.fm (www.fisherman.fm) 33, 84; Peter Goda 45, 77, 81, 92; Eva Greitemann
96; Margarita Hailer 56; Anita Ketterl 78; Leutenegger © Ateliers et Presses de Taizé,
F–71250 Taizé-Communauté 63; Felix Löwenstein 67; Jerônimo Lauricio 12, 30, 66, 93;
Fr. Leo Maasburg 10; Elianne Makhoul 16, 29, 46; Platytera, Greek Orthodox Church, Alte
Schule 3, 51645 Gummersbach, Germany, Icon writer: Konstantinos Chondroudis 80;
Schnorr von Carolsfeld, Creation of the World 20; Reinisch-Sekretariat Vallendar 43; Luc
Serafin 20, 36, 102; Gerhard Weiss 75; Kathleen Wolfe 53

Open source:
Wikimedia-Commons: Creative Commons License by-20 (creativecommons.org/licenses/
by/2.0/): Jon Worth 17; Creative Commons License by-sa-3.0 (creativecommons.org/
licenses/by-sa/3.0/): Reysanchez 40, Paweł Strykowski 42

YOUCAT.org

http://youcat.org/   c   Q▾ Google

About the Church

I believe

YOUCAT Video

YOUCAT Study Groups

Study this Catechism!
This is my heartfelt desire...
Form study groups and networks;
share with each other on the Internet!

POPE BENEDICT XVI
Foreword to the YOUCAT

www.youcat.org

KNOW. SHARE. MEET. EXPRESS.

> Information and ideas on the YOUCAT
> Regularly updated witness by young people
> Study groups for learning about all aspects
  of the Catholic faith
> Creative portal for film, music, artwork, etc
> And much more besides...